Susy,

D0946260

TAKE CENTER STAGE

BE THE STAR OF YOUR OWN STORY

Keep shining You light!

JANELLE ANDERSON

Janelle Anderson

Take Center Stage

Copyright © 2022 Janelle Anderson All rights reserved.
Take Center Stage – Be the Star of Your Own Story

Paperback ISBN: 978-1-953806-77-2
Hardcover ISBN: 978-1-953806-78-9
eBook ISBN: 978-1-953806-76-5

Library of Congress Control Number: 2021923633

No part of this book may be reproduced in any form, including photocopying, recording, or other electronic or mechanical methods—except in the case of brief quotations embodied in articles or reviews—without written permission by the publisher.

All website links were active at the time of printing.

Editing by Kingsman Editing Services
Interior Design by Amit Dey
Photography by Kristina Rose

Published by Spotlight Publishing™ - https://spotlightpublishing.pro
First Edition September 2021

www.emerginglifecoaching.com

TAKE CENTER STAGE

BE THE STAR OF YOUR OWN STORY

JANELLE ANDERSON

Spotlight PUBLISHING
Goodyear, AZ

Take Center Stage Endorsements

"This wonderful, inspiring book gives you a blueprint for happiness, success and a good life. Read it, apply it and let these ideas change your life."

Brian Tracy,
Author/Speaker/Consultant

In a world of so much confusion and darkness, this book shines a light on the path to truth and freedom! Take Center Stage emerges on the scene exactly when we need an authentic, encouraging, and hopeful message that speaks straight to the heart. A must-read for any woman feeling stuck and directionless!

The opening grabs your attention, and you realize that if Janelle can do it, I can do it! It's a rally cry for all women who want to make a profound difference in their life!

The transparency and honesty make you feel like you are part of the story.

Susie Carder,
Profit Coach, Soul Sister, Author of *Power Your Profits*

If you are searching for the motivation and inspiration to break free from old habits of thinking and patterns of behaviors that are keeping you stuck in a rut, this book is for you! It is not only going to energize you with hope, but it also will give you a stunningly clear path to self-discovery with a 4-step process that empowers you to peel away layers of self-doubt and reveal your strong, confident self.

Iman Aghay, Leaders Mentor

Refreshingly honest and straightforward, this book is truly a gem for any woman on a quest to discover her true potential. If you're looking for a blueprint for personal growth and transformation, look no further! Take Center Stage delivers that, and so much more! I wish I'd had this book when I was going through my midlife transition!

Jill Lublin,
4x Best Selling author and international speaker,
master publicity strategist JillLublin.com

Stop! You have just picked up something that can and will literally change your life. I am not being dramatic. I am being honest. Take Center Stage will tug at your emotions as Janelle shares her empowering story and her journey that followed while pulling together a tested and real process to help you with your own. If you are tired of playing small and are ready to take action on creating the rest of your life and emerge as a star, begin reading this now!

Jeffrey St Laurent,
Entrepreneur & Proud Father, SellingCoaching.com

Janelle courageously takes us through her personal journey while also giving concrete steps to taking center stage in your own life. If you are looking for a blueprint for making significant change in your life and turning "one day" into today, this is the book for you!

Angela Lussier,
CEO and Founder, Speaker Sisterhood

What an incredible journey this book takes you on! The stories were moving and resonated deeply with me as a woman working through my own complicated life changes. Janelle lays out a logical and comprehensive process for you to work through, and I greatly appreciated that from a coach's perspective. I loved how her spirit shines through and guides you like a cherished friend. You feel an instant connection to her, and the other women featured along the way. This book is a must-read for women preparing for their second act!

Alexandra Southworth-Molchan,
SPHR, ACC Executive Coach &
Director of People Strategies & Development

"Do you know how great you are?" In this profoundly touching and encouraging book, Janelle shares her story of moving from trauma and a place of deep pain and self-loathing to living a life of peace, confidence, inspiration, and strength. This book is a must-read for every woman who has ever questioned their worth in this world. Discover how you too can give birth to the shining, magnificent, brilliant STAR that you are!

Rev. Lee Atherton,
Founder and Coach, CoachRev @the CrossRoads

Janelle Anderson takes readers on an incredible journey to the inner world. A must-read book for anyone struggling with embracing courage.

Joanna Dziekan,
Spiritual Counselor & Transpersonal Researcher

Janelle is a dynamic individual whose story and wisdom came to life in "Take Center Stage." With great vulnerability, she reveals not only her story of finding freedom, but she empowers you to find the inner strength of discovering your unique journey in fulfilling your destiny. You will not only be able to articulate your past, but you will be positioned to choose liberty in who you were created to be. You can feel the excitement as you read and prepare to launch from your past as a stage to see activation in your greatest aspirations. This book is a must have, it It's time, you have earned it, Take Center Stage.

Tullio O'Reilly,
Executive Pastor, Dwelling Place NRV

As women we have often felt that we need to be people pleasers which creates a barrage of emotions inside of us, such as shame, guilt, remorse, and unworthiness. Janelle bares her soul in *Take Center Stage: Be the Star of Your Own Story*. She shares her STAR process that will enable you to live authentically and create your new story. Janelle shares scripture that touched her life and helped her to heal. The steps she outlines are simple to understand and takes some deep soul-searching to move through the steps. Her 7 steps to forgiveness, will change your life, and help you to understand what true forgiveness is so that you can move forward. This is a must read for any woman that is ready to step into the next chapter of her life.

Cindy J Holbrook,
The Visibility Wiz, Author of Overcoming
Dark Family Secrets

DEDICATION

This book is dedicated to my precious and amazing daughter, Shana—the joy of my life, a true gift from God. Without you, I don't know how I would have made it through the darkest days of my life. You taught me how to love again and gave me a reason to press on and believe that anything is possible. Your love for people—especially those who are hurting—your sense of justice and fairness, your thoughtful acts of kindness for everyone you meet, and your incredible ability to nurture all your friendships no matter where they live in the world have never failed to inspire and amaze me. Thank you for believing in me and being my biggest supporter, helping me to speak my truth. You are the best part of my story.

$\mathcal{A}$CKNOWLEDGMENTS

I want to start by saying how grateful I am to my family for their love and support always. Without them, I wouldn't be here today. In remembrance of my oldest brother, John LeDoux, who wrote letters of hope to me during the hard years in Vegas. Those letters were lifelines for me. Also, in remembrance of my mom, Betty LeDoux—who is now in heaven—for being only a phone call away when I needed her most. Her compassion and kindness wrapped me up in a warm embrace, and I was able to believe in myself because she believed in me. I want to thank my dad, Jack LeDoux, for being the example and leading the way. You've been my foundation throughout my life and have shown me what it means to stand up for truth and speak out because it matters. Thank you for believing in me.

I want to thank my coach, Jeffrey St. Laurent, for helping me early on to get this book started, helping me with setting up the structure and timeline to get it done. It took a bit longer than expected, but here it is.

I want to thank Shalene Massie for the use of her wonderful and cozy Airbnb rental. It was the perfect place for a writer's retreat and helped me get unstuck and into the "zone."

Thank you to Kathy Mikkalson and Shana Thompson for being my test readers and giving me great ideas before sending it off to the editor. Thanks for also cheering me on to the finish line.

Thank you to my amazing clients who have allowed me to share some of their stories: Marguerite, Kathryn, Suzanne, Megan, and Tina.[1] Your commitment to your personal growth and to taking your center stage has been inspiring for me, and it's been an honor to be part of your journey.

I want to say thank you, from the bottom of my heart, to the people who walked with me through the most difficult parts of my past and helped me find my freedom and truth: Rick Sizemore, who taught me how to truly forgive and to know my value and worth; Loretta Crouch, for her faithful friendship, prayers, and unconditional love; and Kathy Tangalakis, who helped me go right to the root of my deepest wounds so they could finally heal. Without your help, this book would not have been written.

I want to thank my sweet daughter, Shana, for being my constant support and biggest cheerleader. Thank you for always being honest and for standing up for truth. You've inspired me to see things from different perspectives to better understand the bigger picture. You've always been wise beyond your years. Thank you for helping me get the words out of my head and onto paper.

And finally, thank you to my wonderful husband, Bob Anderson. You have been my rock through the years, helping me to heal and emerge fearlessly as who I truly am meant to be. You've always seen the best in me, even when I wasn't letting her out. Your steadfast support and encouragement gave me the courage to step out there as myself, on center stage, because you loved me just the way I am and helped me to believe that I can do anything I set my heart and mind to do. You've given me wings to fly!

---

[1] Some names have been changed.

FOREWORD

As a teenager I had really low self-esteem. I didn't like who I was. I had no confidence, I played small, felt fat and unlikable. Growing older into college, all I wanted was to have a girlfriend and to feel loved, yet it seemed to never happen.

If you could have heard the thoughts in my head and what I said to myself... no wonder I felt the way I did. My negative self-talk was horrible.

One day after being embarrassed the night before in a contest to see who could do the most pushups in my college dorm room, a friend asked me if I wanted to go to the gym with him.

With much resistance I said "sure," as I knew it would be good for me but was scared out of my mind. What happened over the next few months literally changed my trajectory in life.

My body began to transform and so did the way I was thinking. I became aware of the mind body connection which I would describe as: the way we feel influences how we think and the way we think influences the way we feel.

From college I went on to owning a personal training business and became a leader in the fitness industry with a career spanning 15 years. I was featured on dozens of educational fitness DVD'S distributed around the world and had the opportunity to work at the Nike world headquarters and Microsoft where I was featured on Xbox One Fitness.

Having helped so many people with their physical health I was looking to grow and find new ways to help people, craving to now work on the mental/emotional health and the behaviors that created them.

This led me to attend the Institute for Professional Excellence in Coaching (iPEC) in 2003, which through this school, fourteen years later, I connected with Janelle.

In those fourteen years after graduating before I met Janelle, I opened my own seminar and coaching company. Authored a book as well as four other personal and business development audio training programs and have devoted over 15,000 individual coaching hours with clients.

This has allowed me great insight into human behavior and why we do what we do. Which ultimately led my transition to becoming a mentor coach, specifically helping coaches transition to a full-time business.

When Janelle came to me she wanted to launch her coaching business. Like most coaches I work with she was full of fear, didn't know what to do and wanted some guidance. Yet under all that fear there was something clear about her intention.

She decided she had enough of that fear and playing small. She was ready to fully step into this and emerge fearlessly and embrace who she was so that she could help other women with their journey.

That set the two of us on a path of launching her business together where we worked closely for over three years. It's in the trenches of the real work that I learn tons about someone. Who they really are. What they truly value. You see, our true character shows when faced with adversity.

Launching a business is no joke. Entrepreneurship will eat you for breakfast, lunch and dinner then snack on you at night for fun. Through it all, Janelle never wavered with her intention. There were hard moments along with highs and lows. Through it all she has impressed me and continues to do so even though I am not easily.

Everyone has great intentions, yet the majority never follow through. Being consistent is hard. Being consistent over time is even more challenging. Not only was it her willingness to do the work, no matter how hard it was for her personally, but after many, many conversations over the years, I began to really understand her methodology and see the results she was creating for others.

She would share with me what she was doing with her clients and their results were real. I developed a deep respect for who she was, what she overcame and how she was channeling that in her work with her clients, programs and first book.

Then in a session she told me she wanted to write another one. As the idea began to unfold I could see this book was different than anything she had ever done. She was even more meticulous and intentional with everything she was putting into this book... like never before!

Now that I have read the final product, what she has put in this book is her whole heart. She really opens up and is vulnerable but not for the sake of being so. For the hope that you can clearly see how broken inside she was and how over three to four decades of hard work, she has emerged into the woman she is... only so that you, the reader, can begin or continue this journey for yourself to discover the star that lives within you.

The four-phased STAR process that she shares truly does help! I have personally seen how it has unfolded results with her clients over the years and developed into this process she shares here now.

A process where you can create your own confidence... a fearless confidence that allows you to pursue your passions and dreams without holding back, without worrying what other people think of you to show up fully on the stage of your life as yourself!

This book will open your eyes to what it really takes to create real changes in your life. It has practical exercises rooted in experience that are wrapped up and presented in a very loving, supportive, and encouraging way.

Make no mistake though, it will not be easy, and you will require help. Just like I did, Janelle did and all the others who have set out on this journey. This book can be your first real tool and then as you begin to implement her process and teachings into your life, I know Janelle will be there for you. Should you desire help, I encourage you to reach out!

As I read through this book I was drawn in because it reminded me of so much, I have gone through with my journey and the work I have done over the years. I think back to the teenager I shared with you earlier and how trapped in my own circumstances and thoughts I was.

This book reinforced how important this journey was for myself, Janelle and is for you right now. Taking the first steps or continuing on from those you have taken is paramount and I congratulate you for getting this far.

I am delighted you are about to learn from someone I would call a master at their craft... so get on reading... your life is waiting!

Take The Leap!
Jeffrey St Laurent
Entrepreneur & Proud Father
SellingCoaching.com

TABLE OF CONTENTS

Scan this code to Access the
Star Guide Workbook

or follow these links to Access
the Star Guide Digital Workbook:
https://bit.ly/StarGuideWorkbook
or the
Paperback Star Guide Workbook:
https://amzn.to/3JUkchQ

INTRODUCTION

The year was 1976. I was twenty-three years old. Sitting at a bar, in a mostly deserted casino in the lull of a Las Vegas midafternoon, I tried to calm the queasiness in my stomach. *What am I doing? Why am I doing this?* My heart pounded in my chest while the urge to run raced through my veins. I looked around for a way of escape, but then I spotted him standing near the door. He was watching me, making sure I followed through with the plan. I knew I was trapped. This seemed to be a dream come true for him, but to me, it was the beginning of a descent into a dark hole that would last for years.

I didn't sit there for long. Soon a paunchy man smelling of booze and cigarettes approached the bar and sat down. He ordered a drink and turned to me.

"Are you working?" he asked.

Resisting the urge to throw up, I answered, "Yes."

We decided on a price and went to his small, dingy motel room not far from the bar. Something switched off deep inside my soul. I went into hiding—my true self, I mean. It would be my survival technique for the next three years as this scene was repeated countless times. Decades later, I learned that this survival technique had a name—disassociation. All I knew was that I couldn't be present for what was happening to me.

It was over in less than twenty minutes. I got out of there as fast as I could. He was waiting for me back at the casino, this man who claimed to love me. On the way home, he excitedly asked me how it went and talked about how great things would be now that I would easily make a lot of money for us. I could almost hear the prison doors slam shut around my heart. I withdrew deeper inside. Outwardly, I submitted to this new life.

That was the day I became a prostitute. No one talked about sex trafficking at the time that I remember. What I did know was that I had become a Las Vegas "working girl." The shame of that label branded me as "ruined" in my mind and heart for more than three decades.

Fast forward to 2006. I was fifty-three years old. Suddenly I was alert, as if I had just awakened from a long, deep sleep. I hadn't known I was asleep. Alive, but not awake. Still a victim to my long-ago buried past, my heart remained shrouded by the shame. Though many years had passed, my true self remained hidden.

My pastor had drawn a simple diagram of a winding road on a marker board as he shared his belief that God has a destiny for each of us as we journey on this earth. We've each been created with a purpose and gifts to share with the world, a contribution that is ours alone to make.

He said, "Just because God has a destiny for you to fulfill in your life, that doesn't mean you automatically will fulfill it! You have a choice to walk that path or to get off the path. It's ultimately up to you whether or not you will fulfill your destiny in this life."

My heart and soul were on fire. Alarm bells resounded in my spirit.

Half a century. I had walked on this earth for half a century, and it felt like a flash in the pan. If the first fifty-three years had gone by that quickly, then the time I had left will also speed by. Now was the time to discover my purpose and fulfill what I am uniquely designed to do in this lifetime. There wouldn't be another lifetime in which to walk that path of destiny. It was crystal clear in that moment that I did not want to get to the end of that path and look back with sorrow and regret realizing that the gift I was meant to leave the world would die with me. This could not happen!

I had a choice. God had my full attention. It was as if He were standing right in front of me, looking straight into my soul, asking me this question: "What will you choose to do with the rest of your life?"

In that moment, I made a declaration in my soul. This pivotal, life-changing declaration would alter the course of the rest of my life and set my feet squarely in the middle of God's destiny for me from this moment forward.

The decision I made that day was simple: I would do whatever it took to discover my true purpose and walk it out. Whatever it took. I would not settle for anything less.

This moment of awakening began a journey of deep, inner healing for me. I had not realized that my twenty-three-year-old self was still sitting at that Las Vegas bar trapped under a load of shame and despair. She needed to be understood and accepted and loved before my fifty-three-year-old self could move forward on her path of destiny.

Something powerful happens when you choose to be free. Everything starts firing inside, and your heart, soul, mind, body, and spirit align. The fog clears and you see your next step. You see opportunities in front of you. Your creative juices begin to flow with new ideas and endless possibilities. Motivation spurs you into action.

My search began in earnest at this point—who am I truly at my core? Who is that young woman still crying for help and desperately searching for forgiveness, acceptance, and love? How did she end up sitting on that barstool and all the barstools that followed? And what is my destiny now? How can I become whole again?

Those questions ultimately led me to discover that I am more than enough. I am uniquely gifted and designed to empower and develop women to be their truest selves. I was sixty years old when I finally found this pot of gold at the end of my rainbow. It was a seven-year journey from my wake-up call to when I knew my calling was to coach and mentor women.

Along the way, I discovered that my past does not define me, but rather it is the stage on which I stand to declare my truth. I discovered how to stand fully in my own light, unashamed and unafraid because I am a daughter of God. He has redeemed me from the shame of my past. He rescued me and plucked me out of the world that had become like quicksand, sucking the life out of me. As I allow God's hand to guide my own, I can share my story with confidence and passion. I can write my new story, the one I will live now and into my future.

I have become comfortable with myself as I am and who I am becoming every day. I am finally at home in my own skin. I embrace and accept all that I am with no more shame or fear. I can look myself in the eyes every day and say, "I love you."

I no longer shrink into the shadows. I am no longer dimming my light. And neither should you! I stand now in the spotlight as the star of my own story, unashamed and unapologetic. I want to help you do the same.

I don't say this arrogantly, but rather with the utmost humility. I am in love with who I am because I know that I am not my own. I am a creation of the one true God, bought with a price and redeemed from the sin of my past by His only Son, Jesus. I am standing in this place today because of His grace and mercy. I know I am amazing because He made me that way. Every single human on the planet is amazing because we were all created in His image and likeness. But our light has been dimmed and covered up with lies that we have believed about who we are, weighing us down with shame and fear.

That day in church, when I woke up, I intuitively sensed that I was embarking on a journey of inner healing. There would be work on my part to break those chains of shame and rise from the ashes of my stolen youth. It would take time and intention, but I made the choice, consciously. I was ready. And that was all God needed from me. He just needed me to say yes.

This choice of stepping out on center stage to stand in your light is no joke. It's not a quick fix. It takes time. It is a journey. It may not take you as many years as it took me, but it will take time, intention, and a willingness to be open and transparent, and even vulnerable at times. I hope that my story and this book will help you make that choice.

It is not the destination that matters. It is the journey—the process of learning who you really are, accepting who you really are, and fully embracing it. This is what truly matters. Your purpose will rarely appear suddenly at the end of the journey. Rather, your purpose unfolds along the way.

The journey is where the treasure lies. If you try to rush it, there will be no unfolding of your purpose. I've seen this play out over and over not only with my own journey but also in the lives of the amazing women with whom I have had the privilege to walk alongside as their life coach.

As I poured over thirty years of journal pages in preparation to write this book, a four-phased process emerged. I call it the STAR Process. I share it with you now with the hope that you will also discover the star that lives within you, your true, beautiful self.

Each phase is divided into chapters that outline the steps along the path. The downloadable STAR Action Guide that accompanies this book provides practical exercises to help you make real changes in your life. This process is transformational, but only when you implement and integrate these steps into your life. Otherwise, it will just be another book and perhaps a fascinating story. That is not my intention in writing this book.

Honestly, it has taken me decades to tell my story. I don't tell it just to tell it. I am sharing it so that other women may also emerge fearlessly from whatever keeps them from fulfilling their destiny. I hope and pray that this will be your experience as you read this book and work through the STAR Process. I urge you to take your time. Work through these exercises prayerfully, thoughtfully, and with a full heart. Be engaged in the process. Please don't just read the book. Experience it.

The STAR Process

Stir Up Your Soul: This is the part where you wake up and become aware of where you are on the path of destiny. This is the time to say yes to yourself and your unique destiny. Chapters 1 and 2 explore this phase.

Tell the Truth: We go a little deeper here, an excavation of the soul in a way. You must bring to the surface the hidden beliefs that hold you back. You cannot be free without knowing the truth. You can't know the truth without uncovering the lies that have entrenched themselves in your subconscious. In this phase, we talk about truth and lies, the power of forgiveness, getting free of shame, guilt, and fear, and how to write your new story of truth. Chapters 3-7 take you through this leg of the journey.

Accept & Activate: This phase is twofold. Once you have cleared out the lies, limiting beliefs, and have discovered your truth, you are ready to embrace the real you. In this phase, we dig for treasure, the treasure of who you truly are and have always been. We look at the hidden pearls of your difficult seasons and how you've overcome obstacles. We discover your unique design and what makes you truly special. This leads you to true self-acceptance, which brings peace and joy and the incredible power of loving yourself unconditionally. Then, you naturally move into activation because the fires of passion and motivation are ignited, and you begin to see all the possibilities ahead. You'll discover your purpose and create a vision of what you want to achieve and who you want to become. Hope arises as you realize all the goodness that waits for you! Chapters 8-10 will cover this phase.

Release the River: Now it's time to release the floodgates of all that you are! Your true self is a force that flows like a river from within you out to the world. In this phase, you are stepping out onto center stage as a star, the full embodiment of who you are created to be. Here you experience the natural flow of releasing your gifts to the world and making the impact only you can make. Everything converges into this life force as you take your rightful place, standing confidently in your truth. Chapters 11 and 12 is where this all happens.

Each chapter begins with an excerpt from one of my journals. I have walked for over forty years as a Christian, a follower and lover of Jesus Christ, who rescued me and loves me unconditionally. My journals are filled with messages He has spoken to my heart. I could not tell this story in any other way, and although this book is not meant to be a book only for Christians, it is filled with God and scripture. I don't know where you are spiritually or what you believe. I'm not here to convince you to believe the way I do. However, I have to be true to my own story and experience, so I allowed this book to flow from a place of authenticity and truth. Whether or not you are a Christian, the principles shared in this book will work for you. They are universal truths and contain incredible power. I hope that my story and the process I share in these pages will bring freedom to anyone who reads it.

With that being said, let's begin.

Scan the QR Code above to watch my special
Welcome to the Journey message for you, or follow this link:
https://youtu.be/FrpeqtoeHpk

PHASE ONE:

STIR UP YOUR SOUL

Scan the QR Code above with your smartphone
for a special message about
Stirring Up Your Soul, or follow this link:
https://youtu.be/Gyk607Y4vAY

CHAPTER 1

WAKING UP

The time is now. Stop hitting the snooze button on your life.

~Mel Robbins

Awake, awake; put on thy strength, O Zion; put on thy beautiful garments.

~Isaiah 52:1

FROM MY JOURNAL (AGE 53)

It's an awakening. A waking up from the deep slumber of being unaware of who you are. A shaking off the dust of this world and what it has thrown on you. Arise to shine in your God-given light and throw off all that holds you back. It's standing in truth—the truth of who God says you are—without apology or shame.

T he first step in the STAR Process is to stir up your soul. That starts with waking up. And it doesn't just happen to you. You choose it.

I Came Alive

When I wrote the above entry in my journal, I was experiencing a deep stirring in my soul. It was like those first few moments in the morning when you are coming out of a deep sleep. A fog lifted from my mind, and just as the sun dawns on a new day, a glimmer of light rose in my heart where there had been obscurity. My soul stirred and awoke, and I became aware of where I was in my life's journey. I had been asleep, but it was time to be here now, to come alive and show up, to be engaged and intentional and purposeful.

Since then, as I have worked with many women as a coach, I have seen this soul-stirring awakening also happen to them. These women inspired me to write this book as a guide on this path, to reveal the markers along the way. One of these women was Suzanne.

Suzanne felt like she was living in a perpetual *Groundhog Day*. Every day was the same as the one before, like she was plodding along in line behind everyone else, robotic and lifeless. She desperately wanted to make a change in her life, but it seemed like it was just too late. She was too old. She didn't have the spit and fire she used to have. Life was a heavy blanket weighing her down.

As Suzanne began to look deeply at her life, she realized that she had walked away from everything that made her alive and peaceful because she neglected herself as she focused solely on caring for others. She had lost herself in the process.

As this revelation unfolded before her, this brave woman knew she had work to do. And this work would be an inside job. Suzanne was waking up.

What Do I Mean by "Waking Up"?

Have you ever driven somewhere, and when you arrived, you were surprised because you didn't even remember driving? Many people live their lives that way, kind of sleepwalking through their days, weeks, months, and even years. It's like you're on autopilot, doing things the way you've always done them, not really being present. Then one day, you realize how much time has gone by, and you wonder where it went. Each day feels the same, and even when something new comes along, there's only a momentary sense of happiness. The excitement quickly fades, and what was once fresh and wonderful becomes routine and mundane. You find yourself living for the next vacation, but even that leaves you feeling empty at times.

That's how Suzanne felt. She was going through the motions. She wasn't experiencing fulfillment or satisfaction in her work, her marriage, her social life, or in herself. But, when she reached out to me, she was beginning the waking-up process. She had begun to stir her soul.

Waking up happens when you stop pressing the snooze button on your life and decide to do whatever it takes to come alive again. It's when you say yes to you and drop the baggage you've been carrying around, probably for years.

Waking up to your life means that you become self-aware. You go inward and honestly look at what is going on inside your heart and your mind. You stop doing what you've always done, mindlessly moving through your life. You stop reacting and you start responding in a conscious, mindful manner.

You start thinking about what you're thinking about.

You ask yourself questions like: Why am I feeling this way? What is triggering me? What am I thinking? Why am I thinking that way? What am I believing about this situation that is causing me to react this way? How do I want to respond? What is important right now? What really matters?

It's an Inside Job

About the time I turned fifty, I took these notes from a sermon by Pastor Keith Johnson that I heard in church: "Changing inside of you is first, then outer change occurs. It's all about an inside work. We don't run after success; it comes to us like a magnet as you work on your inner self. We're so busy doing, we forget the being. Everything created started with a thought. You can tell how big a person thinks by the life he or she creates. Your level of living will always stop at your level of thinking. Success in life comes when you begin to think like God thinks. You can't out-dream God."

You must commit to the inside job before you will see the outer changes in your life that you desire. This waking-up period of my life became a time of understanding *me*—looking at who I really am and how my life experiences have impacted and shaped me.

It was a time of soul-searching and inner healing. It was all about building my confidence in who I am and knowing my worth and value as a person and a daughter of God. It was about knowing my purpose and destiny in this life on earth. I began to clearly see my path and the passion of my heart. That's when things began to fall into place and I knew, without a shadow of a doubt, that I would discover my mission.

Waking Up Starts with Self-Awareness

Awareness is the foundation for change. The Chinese philosopher, Lao-Tzu, said, "Know yourself and you will win all battles." Knowing yourself is the first step to *being* yourself.

Awareness is the first step in living the life you were meant to live. It is especially important to be completely aware when you go through major transitions in your life, such as midlife. When you are aware of what is happening around you and within you in every moment, you have the powerful ability to choose to either continue doing what you're doing or try something different. Awareness gives you the "sight to see" what is happening, what is real, right now. You are awake.

During my season of awakening, my husband and I were running a family fun center that we had built and invested a lot of time, money, and energy into with the intention that in five years, we would buy out our partners and own it outright. This was to be our retirement business, our dream business.

Only it wasn't my dream.

I was exhausted, overworked, stressed, and unfulfilled. We worked long hours, six days a week, and the business had taken over our lives. Full panic sometimes flooded my entire being. I was on an extremely fast merry-go-round that I could not get off of and that was never going to end. When the thought came into my mind that this was what I was going to be doing for years to come, the earth spun around me, and fear overwhelmed my mind. It was a horrible feeling. I thought, "This cannot be all there is for me. There *must* be more!"

On top of that, I was in the full throes of menopause with every symptom imaginable. Without warning, intense hot flashes burned from my feet up, and in seconds, my body was engulfed. If I didn't rip off all my clothes right then and there, I was going to die. If you've ever experienced hot flashes, you know exactly what I'm talking about.

I was irritable and edgy, often losing patience at the drop of a hat over the smallest things. When my employees were in the office counting money, I raked them over the coals if they didn't have all the bills face up, in one direction, as I had been taught in my days as a bank teller. I once told a customer to get out because she had simply asked if her son could wait in our lobby for a half hour before we opened our doors. I was so rude to her. I remember thinking, "Who is this person? This is not me!" But I had no control over my words and actions. I was a crazy woman.

My only child had just graduated college and moved to California (I live in Virginia). As if this wasn't enough, I had recently experienced a devastating wound from my previous church where I had been in leadership for four years. I was a hot mess.

I hated myself for the way I was treating people. I hated working long hours and the stress of running a business with our investors breathing down our necks. My husband and I were fighting constantly, and I missed my daughter terribly. I felt like a complete failure, totally rejected, and I had no idea why I was so miserable. The music ministry I had been so passionate about for over a decade was suddenly yanked out from under me. I was floundering because I had loved it so much. Leading the music ministry was my highest calling in life, but I had utterly failed. I was running a business I didn't enjoy, and my life was passing by at lightning speed.

One day when I was feeling particularly edgy and cranky, one of our employees tiptoed into the office and played a worship CD. She didn't say a word, but her actions spoke volumes. I had to find my way back to the peace of walking in the Spirit (which means to live and behave in a loving, peaceful manner). Later that day, I mentioned to her that I was praying for God to show me how to walk in the Spirit so I wouldn't be so mean to people all the time. What she said to me stopped me in my tracks and became my lifeline back to peace and sanity.

She simply said, "It's just a choice. He's already given you all you need to walk in the Spirit. You just have to choose it every day."

IT'S JUST A CHOICE!

Stunned by the simplicity of what she said, a light flipped on in my soul. It was just a choice, and I had the power to make that choice. The next morning, I chose to walk in the Spirit. I sat on the edge of my bed upon waking and simply prayed, "Lord, today I choose to walk in the Spirit. Please nudge me any time I am starting to fall back into my old patterns. Nudge me in that moment and wake me up to what I'm doing so I can choose again right then and not hours later."

That is exactly what started to happen. I regularly experienced what I now call "spirit nudges."

One day as I was supervising two of our employees counting down the cash drawer at the end of a skating session, I felt the familiar prickly sensation moving up the back of my neck. I was irritated because they were not putting the bills all facing up and in the same direction as I had trained them. It was as if they were scratching a chalkboard with their fingernails.

My normal, irritable self would launch into an acidic lecture followed by impatient sighs. But not on this day. As that prickly irritation inched up my spine, I became keenly aware of a soft, almost imperceptible nudge in my spirit. It floated up into my consciousness ever so lovingly, tiptoeing into my mind and whispering, "What is more important here? The way the money is counted or these precious people?"

That whisper hit my mind like a thundering lightning bolt. My menopause fog brain cleared instantly, and I saw what I had been doing with my sharp, criticizing tone. Not only did I see it, but I also felt it. The weight of my responsibility and the influence I exerted as their boss washed over me like a tidal wave. I realized that I had a choice about how I show up in my life and how I lead others.

I began to see my employees as valuable and precious human souls who deserve to be respected and honored, rather than just task-doers. Even when I needed to correct or train them, I focused my thoughts on the fact that they were more important than whatever task I assigned to them. I learned how to stop anytime I felt irritated or impatient and check my thoughts before speaking. That short space in time allowed me to calm my emotions and choose how I wanted to respond.

This was a huge step in my waking-up process because I was learning that everything I did, said, thought, and believed was my choice. I had the power to live my life however I wanted. I was not a victim to my circumstances or my hormones. I began to take an honest inventory of every area of my life. Was I living it the way I genuinely wanted?

I knew I didn't want to be the crabby, defensive, hormonal woman who was always looking for what was wrong in life any longer. I didn't want to keep slugging through my days, checking off the boxes on the calendar until they were all gone.

This awakening also brought me new excitement as I realized that I could take the steering wheel and direct my life from this point on. I still had lots of years left, and I could choose right now to thrive instead of merely survive. I could make a difference in the world.

Since becoming a coach, I have noticed that this experience of waking up is common for people in their midlife years. It turns out that the research on this stage of life and development for adults confirms what I have noticed in my clients, who are normally women over forty, just like Suzanne.

Dr. Edward J. Kelly, an entrepreneur, researcher, and facilitator, has studied this stage of life extensively. He suggests that there must be a change in our thinking. "Taking the reins on the third act as opposed to surviving the 'third-age' are very different experiences. In the former, we actively co-create our third act; in the latter we are passive recipients of human longevity. Playing an active role however is not just about 'what we do,' it's also about 'who we are.'"[1]

Life expectancy is at eighty now but projected to be ninety by 2030. We're living an average of thirty-five years longer than our great-grandparents. Jane Fonda called the third act "an upward ascension of the human spirit" in her TED Talk on aging. Jane Fonda also said that our third act is where we can "finish up the task of finishing ourselves."[2]

People often tell me that I look so much younger than I am. I believe that is partly due to good genes (By this book's publication, my dad was ninety-seven years young, still living on his own.), but I also believe it is because I am living a life of passion, meaning, and purpose, making a difference in the lives of others. I am now doing work that I love.

I know from experience that you can redefine yourself, rediscover your passions, and reawaken your calling at any age. You have a lot to say about how you'll experience your second, third, or even fourth acts of life. What will your story line be? You get to choose.

It Doesn't Have to Be About Endings

Laura Carstensen, founding director of the Stanford Center on Longevity, said, "The story is ours to write. Life stages are social constructions. We have the opportunity to rethink life's stages in profoundly novel ways."[3]

You need to be awake, though. You need to be aware of what is going on internally. You must be in tune with yourself. How are you showing up in your life? What beliefs and values drive your decisions? How are you treating people, especially those closest to you? How are you treating yourself?

The practice of asking for those spirit nudges became my normal morning routine. Life was an adventure as I began to transform from the inside out. Several months after the nudge I received during that money-counting session, one of my employees commented to me, "You're much nicer now."

I just smiled and said, "Yeah, I'm so sorry for how I was before! That wasn't really me."

I wrote this in my prayer journal when I was fifty-eight (about three years after the spirit nudges started):

> *The metamorphosis of a butterfly is a picture of the transformation of a soul into a daughter or son of God. The work of breaking forth out of the chrysalis causes growth in strength and might so it can fly in the freedom designed for it. You are called into a season of being hidden in the chrysalis, alone in the wilderness. During this season, I speak to your heart and show you who you truly are. As you receive this truth, you are transformed from glory to glory. You go from strength to strength in this process. I begin to release you back out into the world, transformed as the beautiful daughter you are, showing forth your glory and unique beauty. You are now free to fly—to fulfill your destiny and show forth my glory, drawing others to Me.*

For me, this season of awakening was like breaking out of the chrysalis. It was incredibly transformational. I became the fullest version of myself, as if until this point, I had been forming and incubating, learning and amassing skills and knowledge. Suddenly, I was bursting forth into a new world with wings to fly. There was a sense of freedom, but also rich wisdom to be able to read the movement of the wind. There was a flow to my life and a strength that wasn't previously present.

This is what happened with Suzanne, too. As our time together ended, she told me that she had discovered what her soul was crying out for: peace, love, and forgiveness. She had transitioned from "doing" to "being." She said, "I have become much more conscious and aware of emotions and how I react to situations. I am looking more at what's going on internally, and I have much more awareness of choice and being present in the moment." Suzanne was now awake.

She had let go of many beliefs that no longer served her and were keeping her stuck. Her new outlook on life was that her best days were in front of her. She was a different person. It had been an inside job, and now she was focused and moving toward positive thinking and actions. She officially declared that, for her, *Groundhog Day* was over. She had a plan of action, renewed motivation, clarity about the direction she was headed in, and the confidence to step into it.

STIR UP YOUR SOUL

The same can be true for you. Your purpose crystalizes and converges into a new vision. You awaken to new possibilities. You see your life purpose emerging into a fullness that wasn't apparent when you were younger. You begin to realize that fulfilling your purpose is a birthing process. You are giving birth to the seeds implanted inside your heart. It is a process of breaking forth. It is a deeply spiritual experience.

How can you get here? You will find the answer to that question within these pages. Begin with raising your level of awareness. Think about what you're thinking about. Every day, take time to practice mindfulness. Many people find that meditation helps them become more mindful throughout the day. Others find that prayer and worship combined with meditation on scripture and journaling will reawaken a deep connection to the divinely inspired purpose for their lives. Every person must find the practices that work for them. The key is to intentionally create awareness of your internal life.

Here are some questions that you may find helpful in creating this awareness:

- What thoughts do you think regularly?
- What emotions do you experience in various situations and relationships?
- What are your typical responses to stress and tension?
- What words do you speak over your life and circumstances?
- What are your hopes and dreams?
- Where do you want your life to be in a year? Five years? Ten years?
- What actions are you taking toward those dreams to bring them to reality?
- What stops you from taking those steps?

During this awakening phase, as I began to give birth to long-held dreams and hidden passions, I discovered with amazing clarity what I wanted to do for the rest of my life. I often would say to people, "Now I know what I want to be when I grow up."

But a better statement would be: Now I know *who* I want to be now that I have grown up!

Who Do You Want to Be When You Grow Up?

Just like Suzanne chose to wake up from her *Groundhog Day*, step off the treadmill, and begin to live her life as her true self, you also get to choose who you are going to be now and how you will live the rest of your life. And the best person to be is *you*. This is the best time to discover who you are and embrace what you find in that process. This is the time to step out and break forth.

To increase your awareness and start waking up, try the **Wake Up to Your Life** exercise in the downloadable **STAR Guide** that accompanies this book.

This is the time to wake up! This is the time to say yes to you.

Access the Digital Workbook: https://bit.ly/StarGuideWorkbook or the Paperback Workbook: https://amzn.to/3JUkchQ

CHAPTER 2

SAY YES TO YOU

You always have a choice. You are not a victim to your circumstances—you just think you are. It always comes down to a choice.

~ Viktor Frankl

Behold, I stand at the door and knock: if any man hears my voice, and open the door, I will come in to him, and will sup with him, and he with me.

~ Revelation 3:20

FROM MY JOURNAL (AGE 66)

In Matthew 21, a story is told about a landowner and his vineyards. He planted vineyards and placed people in charge of them to tend to them. As I read this story one day, I saw in my mind a picture of the entire earth, as if from outer space. I saw vineyards planted all over the world, in every nation. The earth was covered completely with these vineyards. Vines grew up on trestles, and they had buds on them.

God spoke this to my heart: I've planted a vineyard in every heart. Every person who has ever lived and is living now has a vineyard of mine planted in their inner being, their soul—even in their DNA. The vineyard holds the potential for each person to be who I've created them to be and to grow to their fullest potential. They have the potential to bear much fruit, the fruit of their fullest, truest selves, to grow to fullest maturity.

But the landowner left. The choice is up to each person to tend that vineyard within and bring forth the fruit in every season of their lives. Many choose another way in life and don't choose to bring forth the fruit for My kingdom. Some try to tend another vineyard, not their own. Some bring forth the fruit from their vineyard but choose to give it away to the work of the enemy. Both choices end in missed opportunities. The opportunities to fulfill their true purpose on earth go unnoticed and unrealized.

To be ready for those opportune times (kairos moments) you must be participating with Me in the work of tending your vineyard. We do the work together. My Spirit shows you the tasks at hand, the steps on your path, so you don't miss the kairos moments.

I call each person by name to tend their vineyard and to fulfill their purpose. I call each one to step into the kairos moments and seasons of fruitfulness. I've provided everything they need to do this work. All it takes is a yes. As each one of My children says yes to this inner work of growing to their fullest and highest potential and yes to walking in their path of destiny, they will find they have all they need, for I am with them all the way!

Your Path of Destiny

That moment I described in the introduction when I became fully awake as I sat listening to my pastor's message about our path of destiny was the moment it became clear to me that no one was going to make that decision for me. I had been operating in a victim mentality, believing that my life was happening *to* me and that someone else was going to decide for me where my path was meant to go.

This was a kairos moment for me. It was my choice. Not my husband's. Not my friends'. Not my family's. Mine alone. Would I tend my vineyard so I could produce the fruit and reach my fullest potential? As that realization sank into my consciousness that morning, I chose to say yes. It wasn't merely a passing thought or feel-good gesture. This was a defining moment, a turning point.

That was almost fifteen years ago as of 2021. Even as I write that number, I cannot believe fifteen years have already passed. It seems like only yesterday. Looking back now, I feel incredibly grateful that I said yes.

I'm talking about making a conscious choice about what you want to create in your life. What direction do you want to go? What do you want to do and who do you want to be?

There is no better time to start living the life you were meant to live than right now! But it does take a clear-minded choice. It's like driving a stake in the ground. There will be storms that will try to take you off course. If your choice is not a firm and unyielding commitment to yourself, then you may find yourself being tossed about by every wind that comes along.

You need to be fully conscious about your choice. There is often an illusion that we think we are making a conscious choice when we are merely following a pattern of thought deeply ingrained in our subconscious much like a rut in a cow pasture.

I made many choices in my life that were clearly not on my path of destiny. Before I was fully awakened, I had assumed that my past was long dead and buried. I was operating under the false belief that choices I had made decades earlier had no bearing on how I was showing up in my life today. But I couldn't have been more wrong.

My past had massively impacted my life, and as I became more aware of this impact, I saw how it was influencing my here and now. I couldn't continue to ignore it and pretend it never happened if I wanted to fulfill my destiny. It was time to open the musty, old rooms in my heart and take a long look at what was inside.

Your past can impact your present and your future. But you don't have to remain a victim to it. You have the power to change its impact by changing how you perceive it, and you get to choose how your past will affect your future.

It was time to go back to that barstool in Las Vegas to understand how I had come to be there. It was time to see my twenty-three-year-old self and understand her, embrace her, and forgive her. In 1976, I was a new graduate from college with a bachelor's degree in elementary education. My dream had always been to be a teacher. However, few teaching jobs were available at that time, and I had not been able to secure a teaching position. My boyfriend asked me to drive him to California because he had no car and wanted to move there. I agreed to go since I didn't have a job, and nothing was holding me there. Why not? It sounded like a fun adventure.

On our way to California, he suggested that we stop in Las Vegas. We had run low on money, so we began looking for jobs. I landed a job as a change girl in a casino, but he remained unemployed. We had been in Vegas for about a month when he asked me one day if I loved him. He strategically chose to ask this question at a moment of vulnerability while we were making love. I said yes, I loved him. Then he asked me to become a "working girl," the term commonly used at that time for a prostitute. Would I do this for him out of love? I hesitated, of course. Why would he ask me to do that?

He then embarked on a daily campaign of flattery and showering affection, compliments, and gifts on me. He said that I was too beautiful to settle for making minimum wage as a change girl in a casino. He said that I was worth so much more than just working an hourly wage job. I could rake in the cash and do it much faster using my physical beauty and selling myself for sex. He was persistent, using his highly developed skills of persuasion, taking advantage of the emotionally vulnerable state I was in and the fact that I was thousands of miles away from the support of family and friends. He was all I had, and he knew it.

For years, I berated myself for agreeing to his horrible plan. What kind of person was I that I would allow myself to be degraded to this level? Why didn't I just say no? The main reason I had stuffed this all away and never processed it was because of the shame I felt in who I was as a woman and as a person.

But now the time had come to understand and forgive myself. I didn't just wake up one day and decide I was a worthless human being only good for pleasing men with my body. Prior events had put me in such an emotional and mental state that I could be manipulated for someone else's selfish ambitions. And he was calculating. He knew exactly what he was doing. He was a master at mind games and emotional manipulation. He had been honing that skill for years. And he had found the perfect victim in me.

I had been primed to be his target. Four years prior, at the age of nineteen, I was drugged and raped. In the next chapter,

I'll share more about that event, but for now, just know that this experience left me feeling like "damaged goods" and set me on a path of one bad relationship after another. I became emotionally and mentally vulnerable. I was desperate to be loved by someone, anyone, and the fear of being rejected and left on my own was greater than the abhorrence I felt by doing what he was asking me to do.

I hated myself for doing it, for saying yes to a life that repulsed me. I felt like I was a piece of trash, and my only purpose in life had become pleasing men with my body. This wasn't the way I wanted to live my life. Every time I shed my clothes and engaged in this intimate act with total strangers, I felt demeaned as a person. The act of sex had become just that—an act. There was no relationship, no love, no meaning. With each encounter, I disconnected from my true self and shut down emotionally more and more. I started heavily using cocaine and pills to escape my reality and numb my mind and emotions. Over the years, I often wondered how I got to this place—how did I let my life become this hell? I was raised in a loving family, and I believed in God. I had been taught to respect myself, and yet here I was.

I was afraid to stand up for myself, afraid to speak up, afraid to resist, afraid to make my boyfriend angry, afraid I would be alone. The longer I did it, the more trapped I felt. How could I get out of it? Where would I go? What kind of job could I get now? I certainly couldn't put this down as work history! I had earned a bachelor's degree in elementary education and always wanted to be a teacher, but how could I do that now? I was convinced that this was now my lot in life and there was no way out.

But I was wrong.

There is always a way out, and it was all up to me—I just had to choose to find the way out and take it. And I did.

One night in mid-January 1980, I hit rock bottom. My boyfriend and I had a terrible argument that ended with me on the floor and him on top of me, choking me until I almost passed out. He was not usually physically abusive, but that night, his eyes glazed over with a look of pure evil. It was as if someone else had taken over his mind and body. I was terrified and helpless under his vicelike grip. But suddenly he came to himself, stopped choking me, and quickly left the apartment to cool down. Shaking and trembling, fear and desperation closing in all around me, I was drowning in my despair. I felt like a trapped animal with no one to help me—nowhere to go.

But there was one person I knew I could reach out to who would be there for me no matter what. My mom. I quickly picked up the phone and dialed my parents' number in Virginia. It was around 10:00 p.m. my time, which meant it was midnight her time. But she answered the phone, thank God.

I don't remember what I said to her, but I know I was sobbing, probably sounding hysterical. It must have ripped her heart out. But she remained calm and began to talk to me about choice.

She said that Jesus wanted me to come home to Him, that He wanted to give me peace. I didn't fully comprehend all that she said, but the word *peace* drew my soul like a powerful magnet. It reached to the core of my being and pulled me in close. It cracked open the thick wall surrounding my injured heart, and as a soothing balm, it seeped in through all those cracks in my armor to cover my deepest hurts with love. Hope rose inside me that maybe, just maybe, I could escape the sinking quagmire my life had become.

I chose to open my heart in that pivotal moment and receive from that fountain of peace. It changed the direction of my life instantly and forever. I knew I was free. I didn't know how, but I just knew something had happened and I was changed.

I felt the Spirit of God enter and fill my entire being. Fear of resisting my boyfriend's desires and demands melted away, and suddenly I felt strong and resolved, established in this new freedom. I had a choice. What a relief! I had the power to choose my destiny, and I knew I would never again go out on the streets.

When he came home that night, he found a different woman than the one he had left broken and sobbing on the floor a few hours earlier. I don't know what he thought when he saw me, but he seemed to recognize that something had changed in me. He seemed confused and disoriented. I told him I was never going to go out and "work" again—I was done with that life. I think he figured that he would be able to continue controlling me and that my new resolve wouldn't last. He'd find a way to get me back out on the streets.

Over the next month, my parents helped me take the necessary steps to leave Las Vegas and move to Virginia. But I ran into one problem after another. It seemed that something was trying to hold me there, and my boyfriend continued to devise schemes to keep me in the grips of prostitution and under his thumb. But nothing worked. One of his schemes was telling me he had gambled away all our money and that I needed to go back out and make more. He tried making me feel ashamed to accept money from my parents to help me move because, after all, I could just go out and make that money in a couple of days. He tried the silent treatment. He tried intimidation. Nothing worked. The inner peace and strength I now possessed were beyond his ability to overcome.

He finally gave up and decided he would move back to his home state of Pennsylvania. We packed everything up and headed out of Vegas. He drove his car and I drove mine. I still remember the feeling of relief and gratitude as I drove over the Hoover Dam just outside Vegas and that city fell away in my rearview mirror. I was finally free. I was going home.

I was rescued, literally, from that pit. I began a new life, but my heart wasn't free because I didn't process any of it. I stuffed it deep inside and tried to forget it ever happened. I spent the next thirty-plus years living in an outer shell of myself. My emotions were still mostly shut down. I didn't come out on the center stage of my life because I didn't want people to know the real me. What would they think if they knew the truth?

But thankfully, as I experienced this soul-stirring in my fifties, I knew that I had another choice to make. I had another opportunity to say yes to me. I had avoided this for so long, but I finally said yes to this healing journey of finding my true self underneath all the lies and shame.

My story is dramatic and perhaps shocking to some. Your story will be different. It is your story, and you get to write it. You have a choice, and you have the power within to determine your path. No one can choose it for you, though people will try to tell you what you should or should not do with your life. They can say what they want—the choice is yours alone to make.

Only You Can Choose Your Path

Perhaps you are where you are now because of the choices you have made, just as my choices had determined my reality. Maybe you have chosen the path that others dictated to you or impressed upon you. You may have been so eager to please others and to be accepted that you agreed with their choice for your life. Don't beat yourself up. You are normal. You made the best choice you could in that moment, based on where you were and what you knew.

But now, it's a new day. It's a new season. The very fact that you are reading this book means that you are ready to choose in favor of yourself, in the direction of your passions and dreams. Take ownership of your power to choose. It is the one thing that no one, and I mean *no one*, can take from you. You may feel helpless and trapped like I did, but you're not. If you open your heart up to all that's possible and believe there is a way, you will find it. Seek and you shall find. Open your eyes and look for your open door. It may come from the most unlikely places. Nothing is too small to consider.

What thoughts keep coming to you that you continue to dismiss because they seem impossible? Grab those thoughts—maybe it is just one thought—and pull them close to you. Look at them. Ponder them. Let them grow within you. Then take the next step, no matter how small. Maybe that step is writing the thought down. Writing things down makes them real.

Maybe the next step is calling a trusted friend or family member who will allow you the space to talk it out, without judgment or advice. Choose someone who will just listen and hold that space for you.

It is significant and worthy of taking the time to mark this moment of saying yes to you, like driving that stake in the ground, claiming your life as your own. Imagine you are standing at a fork in the road. One path will keep you on the same trajectory for your life that you are on right now. The other path will change everything for you.

That path is your path of destiny from this point on, and it takes you toward fulfilling your true purpose, being who you were created to be, and living the life designed specifically for you.

You're standing there, pondering both paths. Take it all in. Tune in to your emotions. What do you feel when you look at the path that keeps you going in the same direction you've been going until now? If you stay on this path, what will you feel, and what will your life look like in a year? Ponder that, write that out, and sit with it.

Now, look down the new path, toward your deepest desires and dreams. What would your life look like, and how will you feel living it one year from now? Where could this path take you? Ground yourself here for a while. Let your imagination take you there and allow yourself to dream and step fully into that place. What would it be worth to you if you choose this new path, your path of destiny?

Don't get bogged down in the details. There's no way to know the future and what will happen on either path. The important thing is to allow your heart to tune in to its truest desires and to get out of your head. Let your heart lead you into your moment of choice.

Your heart knows who you are and where you should go and what you are meant to do. Too often, we get caught up in our thinking, in our logical mind, and we choose in favor of the "shoulds" and the "what ifs" and what makes logical sense. The reality is that when we follow our heart, we always make the best choice.

CHOICE CREATES MOVEMENT

You can choose to stay stuck because of fear of the unknown and the "what ifs." You can also choose to follow your heart, trusting that God is leading you. That choice will create movement. As you move down that path, one step at a time, your way becomes clearer. We don't see the entire picture, only what we need to see to move the next few steps. You must learn to be comfortable with being uncomfortable and not seeing the end of the path. You must trust that if this path is for you, then all you need will appear as you go along.

Life is an adventure, full of mystery and discovery. I believe this is all by divine design. Just imagine how satisfying it will be when you reach the end of your life to know that you followed your path of destiny and fulfilled your purpose on this earth!

Say Yes to You

This could very well be the most important decision of your life. Your relationship with yourself is the most important relationship, after your relationship with God. That's not being selfish or egotistical. It can be if you are centered on always having your way and making yourself more important than other people. This isn't about being self-absorbed, arrogant, selfish, or prideful. This is about accepting and embracing who you are, with all your strengths and weaknesses, and placing a high value on yourself as a human being, a living soul, with a purpose on this earth.

This is true humility: seeing yourself as you truly are and seeing the immense value and worth you possess. Not more important or valuable than anyone else, but also not *less* than others. If we are to love others, we must first love ourselves. If we are to love God with all our heart, mind, soul, and strength, we must value and love ourselves because we are His creation, and He loves us immensely. He puts great value on us.

Saying yes to you means choosing the path uniquely designed for you. It's not only not selfish, but it's the most generous thing you can do for yourself and the people in your life. When you choose your path, you are choosing to take your rightful place in the world. You are choosing to release to the world the gift that only you can give. No one can be you but you. No one can be who you are created to be. No one can give the gifts you are meant to give. No one can play your part, and when you don't play your part, it leaves a space that no one else can fill.

SAYING YES TO YOU IS A GIFT YOU GIVE TO THE WORLD

The moment I pushed the publish button for my first book, *Come into My Garden*, I understood what that meant. That book had been in my heart for a decade, waiting to be released. I thought about it for years but kept pushing that thought away, thinking that there was no way I could write a book. Who would want to read it? Who was I to think I could publish a book that anyone would want to read? But that book was like a living, breathing part of me that kept growing inside me. It was like I was pregnant with it. It gently, persistently kept floating into my consciousness as if to whisper, "Hey, I'm still here! I'm waiting to be birthed!"

Finally, I considered that perhaps I could write it and maybe people would find value in it. I had written an earlier version as a gift for my mom and only printed a few copies. It was just a gift for her and my dad and a few close friends and family. I gave a copy to a friend, and she told me that she was reading it every day as a devotional. She even quoted me on Facebook. That's when the thought came that maybe this was something I was meant to write and publish out to the world.

That was a very frightening thought. Putting your thoughts and your creation out to the world is scary. You must be willing to be vulnerable. It was so scary that it took me another ten years before I published it. But the very moment that I pushed "publish," something shifted inside. I heard in my spirit the words "Thank you."

I stopped and listened more deeply. God was speaking to me. He said, "Thank you. I've been waiting for you to release this gift to the world. No one else could write this book. It is a gift I gave you to create and release. Some people need this book. Thank you for writing it."

Okay, wow! What? In that moment, it felt as if my book sprouted wings and took flight. My heart exploded with joy. It didn't even matter anymore if people would like it or read it. In that moment, and even still today, I am not attached to people's opinions about it or how many sales I make from it. None of that matters at all. It was a gift inside me that I was meant to give. Once I gave it, I was filled with joy and the satisfaction that came from fulfilling my purpose. That was all the reward I needed. And when people tell me how my book has impacted them, how much they have received from it, that is just icing on the cake.

This is what I mean by the gift you are meant to give to the world. There are many gifts inside you waiting to be birthed. Often, people ask me why it's taking so long for God to fulfill His purpose in their lives. I just tell them that they've got it backward. He is waiting for *them*. He is not going to fulfill your purpose for you. He will walk with you, empower you, and equip you to fulfill it, but you must choose it. You must take the action needed to manifest it in your life.

It was like God wrote that book through me, and honestly, it flowed out. But *I* had to start writing. *I* had to put my hands on the keyboard and start typing. Even though the book was in me, I had to do something to get it out of me and onto paper. God was not going to write the book for me. However, once I started writing, I truly felt God writing the book through me, like a river flowing effortlessly out from my heart where it had been living all those years.

When you put your stake in the ground and start taking steps on that new path, you will find that flow as well, carrying you forward. You will see doors open before you and people crossing your path that will help you. Fresh ideas will appear in your mind, resources will come your way, and all that you need will be there when you need it.

Will it be an easy and smooth path? Not likely! There will be bumps in the road, obstacles in your way, mountains to climb, setbacks, frustrations, and disappointments. But when you are on your unique path of destiny, those things won't stop you. They will make you stronger, more resilient, and you will find that they become stepping-stones rather than stumbling blocks. It is in the struggle that you grow. If you look for the gifts in the struggle, you will find gold there.

You don't grow strong muscles unless you have resistance and a little pain. So, instead of fighting against the pain, breathe into it and look for the gold—the lessons, the wisdom, the growth. The feedback you need from those obstacles helps you see new perspectives and gain a new understanding. Challenges and problems are not bad things to avoid or dread. They are part of life along with the joyful and pleasant times. Accept them as they are and ask what the message is that they bring. When you encounter the hard times, seeing them in this light will change everything for you. You will continue to find joy in the journey even when it rains.

FACE THE FEAR AND DO IT ANYWAY

Is it normal to be afraid to say yes to yourself and your dreams? Absolutely! I think we all feel that fear. If we didn't feel some of that shakiness and knots in the stomach, we probably aren't dreaming big enough. I have coached many women over the years, and I have come to believe that our greatest fears are directly connected to our greatest calling and purpose. Our inner critic shouts the loudest when we begin to move in the direction of our deepest passions. It happens to all of us.

Consider this, though. What would be worse: facing the fear of stepping into your dreams and falling a little along the way or looking back at the end of your life at what you could have experienced if you had followed your heart?

"There is freedom waiting for you, on the breezes of the sky, and you ask, 'What if I fall?' Oh, but my darling, what if you fly?" said Erin Hanson, an Australian poet, and she's right. I am more afraid of not fulfilling my purpose than I am of facing troubles and struggles and even failure because I know that I cannot fail. If I fall, I will learn what works and what doesn't. When my daughter was a toddler trying out her new legs, she fell many times. But she kept getting back up until she strengthened the muscles in her legs and learned how to balance. I know that if I keep trying, if I keep pursuing the passions in my heart, eventually I will fly!

So, my friend, here you are standing at the crossroads in your life. Which path will you choose? Are you ready to say yes to you? If you are, I am ready to take the next step with you. Choosing to say yes to you is the first step on the path. Waking up and choosing to say yes completes the first phase of the STAR Process—Stir Up Your Soul. Your heart's passions have been stirred, and the embers have been fueled into a flame burning in your soul. You're motivated and energized and ready to get started on this glorious path of taking center stage in your own life.

PUT YOUR STAKE IN THE GROUND

Celebrate this moment! This is significant and a moment to be marked as a memorial. It's your stake in the ground. You'll want to remember it so that you can recall your why—*why* are you on this path?

Take a moment now and write that down. Create your memorial statement about this decision. Know why you chose your path of destiny. What will this decision change for you? How will your life be different now? What is the significance of choosing you?

You must mark this moment because the next phase is often rocky and difficult. You must be ready and sure-footed to successfully traverse this terrain.

The next phase is the Truth-Telling phase of the STAR Process. This is where it's time to get real with yourself and face the monsters hiding in the closets of your heart. It feels scary, I know. Trust me, I've been there. The monsters aren't real. They can't hurt you.

Before stepping into the Truth-Telling phase, take a break and complete the Your Path of Destiny exercise and your Stake in the Ground Memorial Statement in the **STAR Guide**.

Access the Digital Workbook: https://bit.ly/StarGuideWorkbook
or the Paperback Workbook: https://amzn.to/3JUkchQ

Phase Two:

Tell the Truth

Scan the QR Code above with your smartphone to view
my special Tell the Truth message. Or, follow this link:
https://youtu.be/pHLymaqf8B4

CHAPTER 3

TELL THE TRUTH

If we follow the truth, it will bring us out safe at last.

~ Ralph Waldo Emerson

*And ye shall know the truth, and the
truth shall make you free.*

~John 8:32

FROM MY JOURNAL

I see a walled garden. It is full of lush plants and trees, and vines crawl up the walls and spill over the wall to the outside. Jesus walks along the outside of the wall, standing up on tiptoe to peek over it, looking for the opening into the garden. He finds the gate, and it is unlocked and ajar. His face lights up with a huge smile, and he throws his head back and laughs joyfully. Then he opens the gate and walks into the garden.

He looks around with pleasure at all the lushness and fruits, the beauty, and he breathes in the fragrances. Then he takes some fruit from a vine on the wall and takes a bite. He throws his head back, opens his arms, and shouts with joy. He looks around like he is taking inventory of this garden.

As I look deeper into the vision, I notice that only the area near the gate is clear. The ground is clear, the plants trimmed and rich with fruit. The paths going into the garden don't go very far, however. They go out in all directions for a short distance, then are stopped by thick undergrowth and thorns that cover the plants. Beyond this point, the plants all seem to be covered by something. Jesus takes out pruning shears and other tools and starts to work in one of the overgrown areas. He looks at me and waits, as if to say, "May I go deeper?"

The Truth-Telling Phase

The Truth-Telling phase is a beautiful journey into the truest part of yourself—your innermost being. This is your soul, your heart, your real self. Your soul is the essence of who you are, your core being, that is housed in your physical body. Your spirit is the part of you that connects to God, to the divine Creator. You communicate with Him through your spirit, and your spirit communicates to your soul. It is in your soul where your power to choose resides. Your conscious mind is like the tip of an iceberg, but it operates from the deeper part of you, your subconscious mind. This process starts with trusting your heart and God's heart enough to go deeper into the garden beyond what you can see right now. It starts with looking at the impact your past has had on your life, facing the things you've left unresolved and unprocessed, and telling yourself the truth.

Before we jump into this phase of the STAR Process, allow me to share this acronym with you to help you remember each piece of this phase. This is the longest phase and takes the most self-reflection and honesty. It can't be skipped or rushed through if you really want to take center stage and be the star of your story!

T.R.U.T.H.

T = Trust Your Heart (as you face the impact of your past): The first step in this process is usually the most difficult. It feels so risky, like you're leaping into the great unknown. Trust your wisdom to be your guide. You probably intuitively know that there are things that you need to resolve from your past, but it has seemed too daunting to go there. Trust your heart. Trust your Creator. Say yes to your freedom and commit to dig deeper into the garden of your heart. It's going to be okay. You will come through on the other side, and it will be glorious!

R = Reclaim Your Heart (and uproot all the lies): We'll explore this in the next chapter as we look to uproot the deeply embedded thought patterns that have taken up residence in your heart but don't belong there. Sometimes they are difficult to distinguish from what is true because you have believed them for so long. You've sown seeds in your heart that are not good. These are the lies you have believed or false conclusions you have established about who you are, who others are, who God is, and what your purpose is in this world. The good news is that you have authority over your life through your power of choice. You can remove those toxic thought patterns and reclaim your heart.

U = Unchain Your Heart (through the power of forgiveness): Holding on to grudges, bitterness, and resentment keeps you chained to the person who wronged you. In Chapter 5, we'll take a long, hard look at what forgiveness is and what it is not. I'll show you the two sides to forgiveness that will bring you freedom. I'll share my 7-Step Forgiveness Process that will help you release offenses when you are hurt or mistreated by others. It will also teach you how to forgive yourself, which is probably the hardest thing for most people to do.

I know it was for me. I'll tell you that story later. For now, let me just say that until I saw how heavy the chain of unforgiveness toward myself was, I had no idea the burden I carried around. Imagine being chained to a huge rock on the bottom of the ocean, unable to move, drowning in your self-hatred, but not knowing it. Once you free yourself from that ball and chain, you quickly float up to the surface where you can breathe again. It is incredible. The same thing is true when you forgive others.

T = The Trials of Your Heart (reveal gifts in the wilderness): You may be thinking that this is the last thing you'd want to look at. Who wants to think about your hardships and trials? I get it. If you're like me, you just want to get through it and get it over with so life can go back to normal. Most people just endure difficult seasons and push through to the other side. But have you ever searched for the gold that's there in the wilderness? Treasures forged in the fires of adversity will become part of your strong foundation, your character, and your inner wise woman. There are lessons in the wilderness you don't want to miss.

H = Hear Your Heart's True Story (and let go of the false stories): Wounds of the heart can take time to heal. They can go very deep. They can make it difficult to hear your heart's true story. At this point in the Truth-Telling phase, you've likely uncovered a lot of hidden hurts and wounds, possibly some that have been long buried. They've all carried stories, words that you've spoken over yourself, and they've formed the narrative of your life.

At this point in the Truth-Telling phase, you'll be listening for the story underneath all of that for your heart's true story. The key to doing that is to practice self-kindness. Let go of self-blame and the shame that comes with that.

Speak kind words to yourself. Affirm that you are a valuable, worthy, and lovable person who deserves to be whole and free. Sometimes, we allow our wounds to define who we are, and we become victims. This becomes a person's identity, and everything they do and say flows out of that identity. They become a wounded person constantly needing validation or sympathy. I was that person at one time.

Know this: Your wounds do not define you. They are just the effect of something that happened to you. The most healing thing you can do for yourself is to separate your identity from the things that have happened to you. They are not the same thing. Hurting hearts can feel like there are empty holes inside. Those holes can be filled in again as you practice self-love and self-kindness.

God is love. His very nature is love and He loves you. He knows your heart's true story. When you listen closely, you'll hear it, too. Your heart will heal, and you will see your true story manifest right before your eyes.

Trust Your Heart as You Face the Impact of Your Past

"A garden enclosed is my sister, my spouse; a spring shut up, a fountain sealed."

~ (Song of Sol. 4:12)

I Had Fooled Myself

My heart was locked up tight, shut off so that no one could get in and hurt me again. To the outside world, I appeared to be fine. My wounds didn't show. Most people who knew me had no idea that I was hiding my shame and many dark secrets. In fact, most of my thirty-five years from being freed from a life of prostitution to when I began my process of Truth-Telling, I thought I was living a normal life like anyone else. I had become so good at hiding my past and my shame that I fooled even myself!

I had convinced myself that my past was gone, and if I never talked or thought about it, it wouldn't have any effect on my life. It was in my past, so long ago, so why bring it up? What good would it do to talk about it? What would people think of me anyway? My past was forgiven, and as a Christian, I knew that it was all washed away by the blood of Christ and His sacrifice on the cross. It was all "under the blood" as we Christians say, wasn't it?

Yes, that is true. I completely believe that. I was forgiven and cleansed. The problem was that my wounded heart never healed from the abuse and trauma, and my emotions were still shut down. I was disconnected from parts of myself. This took away my empathy for others because I didn't feel much of anything. It was difficult to establish close relationships because I couldn't open up. It felt like I was always pretending to be someone else. Through all those years, I often felt like I was living on the front porch of my life because my house was a mess inside, and I didn't want anyone to see it. I didn't even want to look at it or clean it up.

When people asked me for my testimony, my story of how I came to Christianity, I usually felt a little panic rise. My mind scrambled for something I could say that was true but without telling the whole story. I would tell a half-story, a half-truth, and it felt very inauthentic and shallow.

I found that I could not experience deep emotions about anything. When I watched a movie that had everyone else in tears, I only felt a little bit. Anytime strong emotion rose in my heart, it quickly shut off, like turning off a faucet. And it wasn't conscious on my part. I tried hard to feel it, to let it come, but it always shut off. My friends would apologize for crying, saying they just couldn't help it, and I would think, "I wish I *could* cry."

This affected intimacy in my marriage, too. I would have flashbacks sometimes, but mostly just a sickening feeling in the pit of my stomach when we became intimate. Over the years, that faded a lot as I trusted my husband's love for me and understood that I was safe with him. He was not using me. I could let down my guard with him and enjoy our time together without shame or guilt. I could rest knowing he truly did love me and was not concocting a plan to manipulate me for his gain. But strong, passionate emotions still eluded me to a large extent—shut away in that locked garden. I was unable to experience them as much as I wanted to.

Running into a Wall

I began to awaken to the realization that I was running into that same wall in worship services at church, too. I could only go so far, and then there it was again—that wall of numbness, of no feeling at all. I began to feel the wonderful peace and presence of the Lord washing over me, filling me with joy and warmth, and then *bam*—I hit the wall and that experience, and the feelings all melted away. I would find myself standing there in this dead space again. All around me others were crying, laughing, and enjoying His presence, and I was standing on the outside looking in, longing to be part of the experience. I tried to conjure up the feelings, to push through the wall and step into that blessed space, but no matter how hard I tried, I couldn't break through. It felt so lonely. I thought something was seriously wrong with me. I was frustrated with myself and jealous of everyone else.

Over the years, especially as a worship leader, I had moments of being caught up in the presence of God and a deep connection with the Spirit. But I came to the place in my mid-fifties, in my season of awakening, where I had a strong sense that there was so much more. There was so much more to living than what I was experiencing—spiritually, emotionally, relationally—and I could no longer tolerate this wall.

THE WALLED GARDEN

It was about this time, one day while in prayer, that I received the powerful vision of the walled garden of my heart that opened this chapter. It was so vivid and clear and carried a message that would become the key to the healing my heart desperately needed.

I knew what He was asking of me. He was asking me to face the trauma of my past. Specifically, the seven-year period from the ages of nineteen through twenty-six when I endured rape, sexual exploitation, an abortion I didn't want, and three years of prostitution. My heart lurched, and the hairs on the back of my neck stood up. I shivered in fear and dread. Oh, Lord, no. Please no! I didn't want to go there. I didn't want to see what was in that thick overgrowth and under all those thorns, in that dark place. I didn't want to think about it or talk about it. Wasn't there another way?

An entire year went by before I finally said yes. I finally gave Him permission to go deeper in the areas of my heart that I had locked away for so long. I was ready. I knew it was time to bring it out into the open, talk about it, look at it all, process what happened, and break the shame off my heart. It was time for healing, for real—deep inner healing.

It was time to tell the truth—to myself. Life wasn't worth much without all of me participating. I desperately wanted wholeness and freedom. I didn't want to be divided or shut down. I wanted to be completely engaged and showing up in my life. I wanted to embrace my true self fully and take center stage as the real me, no longer wearing a mask or trying to fit into a role that wasn't mine. It was time, and I finally said yes.

This was the beginning of a whole new way for me. I had been afraid for so many years that I couldn't process what had happened to me in my younger years. I had been so afraid of feeling all that pain and hurt and shame again. But that fear had kept me trapped and living in the outer shell of myself.

That's what happens to many people. We all have our dark stories, our places of shame and regret, parts of our past we'd rather forget ever happened. Many women, like me, choose to stuff those things away in a deep, dark closet in their hearts without realizing that they don't go away when you do that. You need to open the doors of the closets, bring out all the junk, look at it, process it, and then tell the truth to yourself.

It is a process best done with people who love you and know how to walk through the darkness with you. If you have a lot in there like I did, don't do this alone. Please find someone like a therapist, coach, or minister to guide you and walk with you.

I'm going to share the process I went through to find my freedom, but yours may look different. There is not just one way to do this. There are many different approaches to find your inner truth and healing. The important thing is to do it. You'll never move on without doing this inner work unless you have no unresolved past hurts and issues. But I have never met anyone who doesn't have at least one thing stuffed away in a closet somewhere. It means no one is alone in this journey.

You may have already done this work, and if so, that's awesome! You will know it, too, because you will find yourself easily moving forward on your path toward taking center stage and being the star of your own story. You will be able to fully embrace who you are and feel totally at home in your skin. You will not compare yourself to others or find that you feel inadequate or unworthy of walking in your purpose. You will feel a powerful green light, a go in your spirit, that propels you forward to creating the life of your dreams. I'm right there with you. Good for you that you have done the work and you are walking in your light!

But if you're not there yet, that's okay. You will be. And I'm right here with you. Just know that there's nothing wrong with you. You are normal! You will find your way to the light. The hardest step is saying yes to the process.

Your past does have an impact on your present. You have stored memories from your experiences, and you formed a perspective (a filter) through which you view yourself and the world. These perspectives together with the emotions that you felt have been embedded in your subconscious mind (I call this your heart), and they have shaped a part of your identity. The way you've lived your life, the decisions you've made, and the way you see yourself and others all have been influenced by your experiences.

You may be living according to a set of values that were handed down to you by your parents, grandparents, teachers, and other influential adults in your childhood. You were taught to think, feel, and react a certain way according to your family's upbringing, religion, culture, or traditions. Your past probably has had both positive and negative influences on the way you view the world today. The important thing is not to ignore the impact of the past on your life now but to take the time to dig deeper into the garden of your heart so you can uproot any weeds that don't belong and are choking out the truth of your real self, or perfect self, as Dr. Caroline Leaf calls it. This is your truest self, your innermost being. This is how she describes the "Perfect You": "It is at the core of our being, the particular essence of who we are, laid down in our spirit. It expresses itself through the active mind, or through how we think, feel, and choose. It expresses itself through what we say and do."[4]

She goes on to explain how what we think and how we perceive our world becomes the wiring in our brains, like plants being embedded in a garden. "In other words, your thinking, feeling, and choosing actually create matter. Your physical memories are made of proteins that are expressed by your genes, which are switched on or off by your thinking. These thoughts produce fruit: the words and actions that are exclusive to you are a construct of your mind. Thus, your mind is not only unique but powerful as well, since it has the power to create realities (physical thoughts made of proteins) out of probabilities of perception (thinking signals)."[5]

Can you see why ignoring my past did not work for me? Those physical tracks were still in my brain and my mind. They weren't going away on their own, and they still impacted my life. So, for me, digging deeper into that garden meant going back to places of trauma.

Therefore, the first step in the Truth-Telling phase is to dig a bit deeper in the garden, into your past, to see what might be keeping you stuck. Your past can show you who you are and what has helped you to be successful. Looking at your past doesn't have to be a scary, negative thing. In fact, for most people, it is an enlightening and encouraging thing to see the people who and the experiences that have inspired you and molded you throughout your life.

The conscious mind is like that outer part of the garden. That's where most of us live our day-to-day lives. It's filled with the things we see and think about that are right in front of us—our daily tasks, to-do lists, and the people we interact with every day. The subconscious part of us, our heart, is what drives the conscious mind, even though we're mostly not aware of it. This deeper part of us informs our conscious minds about how we view the world, our lives, and others. Our hearts contain the programming, our system of beliefs and values, that have become our operating system.

Our heart also contains the residue of our past hurts and traumas that have created in us certain conclusions about who we are and how we are to live—and about who God is. These are the places in the garden that are overgrown with thorns and weeds that choke out our true-life source. If we don't clear that out, we will only live in a shell of who we truly are, and we will not ever be completely free.

When I began digging into the past, I imagined it would be like trying to take a huge rubber band ball and disassemble it, one band at a time, to get to the core of it. I thought it was going to take forever and be excruciatingly painful. But I was committed to the process. Whatever it took to find my freedom, I was going to do it.

I was pleasantly surprised to find that it didn't take nearly as long as I thought it would for that rubber band ball to fall apart. For me, this process consisted of a deep dive into a few key events that had deeply embedded lies in my heart, and once I dealt with them, true freedom emerged. After that, it was a matter of reprogramming my heart with the truth and learning to love myself completely, accepting every part of me as a beautiful and worthy person with immense value as a human being, a woman, and a daughter of God.

You may find, also, that this process isn't as scary and torturous as you imagine it will be. Especially if you walk through together with the One who loves you most. I don't know what your spiritual life is like or what you believe about God. I just know my own experience as a born-again believer—that He will walk through your garden with you. He will never leave you nor forsake you. He loves you with an everlasting love, and His loving-kindness lasts forever.

There is nothing you have done or experienced in your life that He won't forgive and cleanse. He knows the deepest hurts in your heart, and He will pour His healing love into those wounds, filling all the empty places. But you first need to say yes. He doesn't barge into your heart and force anything on you. This process is completely gentle, filled with kindness and compassion, and never judgmental, condemning, or critical.

The goal of the Truth-Telling phase is to be firmly established on truth. It starts with looking at the impact of your past, not so you experience all the pain again or be re-traumatized, but to see and acknowledge the truth. In the next chapter, we will explore uprooting the false beliefs that are getting in the way of knowing your truth. Then we'll move on to a deep dive into forgiveness and its power to bring freedom. The next step is to understand the lessons of the wilderness and how your struggles, hardships, and difficult seasons have created a storehouse you can stand on as you take center stage. And finally, we look at how to access your heart's true story and let go of the falsehoods you've believed for far too long.

For now, I encourage you to work on the Weeding Your Garden exercise in the STAR Guide.

Access the Digital Workbook: https://bit.ly/StarGuideWorkbook
or the Paperback Workbook: https://amzn.to/3JUkchQ

CHAPTER 4

RECLAIM YOUR HEART

To heal is to touch with love that which we previously touched with fear.

~Stephen Levine

Keep thy heart with all diligence; for out of it are the issues of life.

~Proverbs 4:23

FROM MY JOURNAL (50 YEARS OLD)

When I was fifty years old, I had a dream. It was one of those dreams that stays with you. It was so vivid and real, and I felt that it had an especially important message for me. I had this dream about five years before I started going through my Truth-Telling phase, and I didn't yet realize how significant the dream would be on my journey.

The Estate Dream

I was coming home from a concert with a group of friends. When we arrived at my home, I realized it was a huge estate that had been abandoned and run down for years. The house was falling apart, and squatters lived on the property. The grounds were filled with them, and they had dug holes in the ground for fire pits. They were very well established and deeply entrenched.

One on the back porch prepared to build a fire. I told him he had to leave, but he said he wasn't leaving. He had been there for years, and this place was open game because no one owned it. I told him that this was now a private residence and he had to leave. He refused and continued building his fire. I called the police, and then I picked up a megaphone and declared loudly to all the squatters that the police were on the way, and they had to leave. This was private property, and they no longer had any right to stay. Many of these invaders cleared out immediately, but they tried to come back. The one on the porch wouldn't leave for a long time.

A couple there were like mentors or guides who helped us know what to do. There seemed to be a long battle getting all these invaders uprooted and removed, but we finally did get the place cleared out and restored.

The atmosphere was filled with overwhelming peace, love, and joy. I had never experienced anything so powerful and fulfilling and deeply satisfying. I couldn't stop crying. Someone took me up on the porch, and all the people there were applauding me. I felt like a celebrity, and they even asked for my autograph. I wrote "God is good!" as my autograph. I felt completely immersed in this flood of total acceptance just for who I was.

The emotions I experienced in that dream stayed with me for years. Even now, I can close my eyes and go back to that moment on the porch and feel that incredible acceptance and love flow through my being again. It wasn't until years later when I had gone through uprooting all the weeds in the garden of my heart that I fully understood the message of this dream.

THE MESSAGE OF THE DREAM

The estate represented my inner being, my heart and soul that had been shut down and in disrepair for years. I wasn't "residing" there. I wasn't present with my true self. I was trying to be someone else without a dark past, someone I thought others wanted me to be. I couldn't settle into my core identity and live from a place of complete acceptance because I couldn't accept myself. And because I abandoned my true self due largely to the shame I felt from my past, these squatters came in and firmly established themselves in my subconscious.

The squatters represented the false narratives I believed about who I was. Some of them were deeply rooted. The battle strategy to clear them out was based on standing in my authority to speak truth over my heart. In the dream, this was represented by calling the police and then using the megaphone to declare it over the property.

This battle raged for some time, but those stories had been entrenched for years. It didn't happen overnight, and my healing would not happen overnight either. This has to do with our thought patterns. They are like ruts in a cow pasture that become deep over time as the cows keep treading the same path. When we think the same thoughts over and over, we embed them in our minds and hearts. Neuroscientists have even discovered that our thoughts create neuropathways in our brains!

Dr. Caroline Leaf is a neuroscientist focusing specifically on the science of thought as it pertains to thinking and learning. She did some of the initial research in neuroplasticity in the 1990s. She said, "You are a thinking being. You think all day long, and at night as you sleep, you sort out your thinking. As you think, you choose, and as you choose, you cause genetic expression to happen in your brain. This means that you make proteins, and these proteins form your thoughts. Thoughts are real, physical things that occupy mental real estate."[6]

As a communications pathologist who specializes in the field of cognitive neuroscience, Dr. Leaf has focused her research mostly on "how humans think and the impact of this thinking on what they say and do." She has studied the concept of free will, and her research supports that free will is real. We have a choice about what and how we think, what conclusions we come to about what things mean, and what we believe.

As Dr. Leaf said in her book, "You are able to stand outside of yourself, observe your own thinking, consult with God, and change the negative, toxic thought or grow the healthy, positive thought. When you do this, your brain responds with a positive neurochemical rush and structural changes that will improve your intellect, health, and peace. You will experience soul harmony."[7]

Thoughts have substance to them. So, to clear out the well-established toxic thought patterns, we need to create new pathways of truth and freedom. I like to think of this process as creating a new sled run in deep, newly fallen snow. It's so much easier to sled down a slick, packed path, isn't it? If you want to create a new path that no one has sledded down before, it will take work and persistence.

That's what happens in our brains. When we think a certain way over time, our brains get used to that thought pattern, and it gets easier and uses less energy to go down that path. Our minds will resist a new pathway at first because it takes more energy and effort. But you can change those thought patterns, which will change your life.

In her book, *The Perfect You*, Dr. Leaf explains, "When we think, feel, and choose, our minds process the incoming knowledge and change the wiring of our brains. So, if we mindfully tune in to our ability to think, feel, and choose by paying attention to our thoughts, we can understand our Perfect You, the very core of who we are—our blueprint for identity. To find out who you are and what you are made for, you have to understand how your mind and brain interact, and you can do this by understanding your thinking, feeling, and choosing."[8]

Where Do Those Squatters Come From?

They often start when we are young. Someone says something to us, or we have an experience and attach a meaning to it, a perception of what it says about who we are, and then we believe it is the truth. We begin to live according to that perceived truth. As children, we don't have the capacity yet to analyze our perceptions and discern truth from a lie, so we just accept our thoughts as truth.

These events from childhood are often ordinary, everyday events. They are not things you would think would cause one of these "squatters" to take root. They are not always caused by traumatic events. What is more important is the meaning you attached to the event, not the event itself.

One of my earliest memories that came up while I was going through my Truth-Telling phase illustrates this very well. I think I was about four or five years old. I was at a friend's house having dinner. Sitting at the table getting ready to eat, I heard my dad calling for me outside. We lived on a naval base at that time and the houses were close together. I wanted to run to my dad, but I was in someone else's house and felt like I shouldn't leave the table, so I just sat there. After a few minutes, my dad stopped calling for me because my mom had told him where I was.

No big deal, right? Nothing traumatic here. I wondered why this memory kept coming up. As I sat with it and asked God what it meant, I began to understand. In my little girl's heart that day, a false conclusion began to take root. It was the feeling of abandonment, of not being worthy or valued enough to warrant my dad to keep looking for me until he found me. Of course, this was not at all true. But in my heart, that was what I felt for just that few minutes and I attached a meaning to this event—that I wasn't important enough. I was not worth pursuing. It was a small idea planted in my subconscious mind, my heart. It was a seed sown there, to be watered later by other events where that same lie became a truth for me.

I do believe there is an enemy of our souls that whispers these lies to us. The Bible calls him the devil. You may not believe in the reality of the spiritual realm, but I do. The Bible tells us that he is a liar, and his mission is to steal from us, kill us, and destroy us. He does this through lies, insidious whispered little lies spoken into our hearts as children. We believe them and they begin to take root. They become our inner critic. Whether you believe there is a devil or evil spirits or not, all of us experience these lies embedded in our souls at some point in our lives. They become the roots that establish the "squatters" in the land of our hearts.

These roots often consist of three major emotional components: fear, shame, and guilt. They show up as signposts in our journey of reclaiming our hearts. When we stop to find the source of these emotions, we'll discover the messages deeply embedded in the soil of our hearts, such as "I am not good enough. Something must be wrong with me. I am not acceptable as I am." This is the soil of our soul's identity, and if it is filled with those toxic beliefs, the fear, shame, and guilt will flourish and grow strong.

THREE EMOTIONAL COMPONENTS OF OUR "SQUATTERS"

Fear—makes you shrink back and play small. Marguerite found herself with an empty house, an empty nest, and paralyzed by fear. A creative and outgoing woman, she intuitively knew that there was more for her to do in her life beyond raising her children and taking care of her home. She loves being with people and creating beautiful things that will bless others. When she sought me out as her coach, she was already doing that through her sewing circle.

Marguerite operates a ministry called Sew for Souls where she gathers women together to create beautiful items like pillowcase dresses for little girls in third-world countries and zippered pouches to hold personal items for women who have escaped abusive situations and are living in shelters. This ministry gives her much satisfaction, fulfilling both her desire to create and her love for connecting with people and helping those in need.

But Marguerite felt stuck. She was filled with the desire to learn and grow personally. She knew she was meant for more, but she was being held back by fear. She was afraid to venture out and apply for a job. She was afraid to sign up for classes to learn new things and acquire new skills. Her fear was rooted in her belief that she was not good at learning, especially when it came to technology. The learning struggles she wrestled with her entire life created deep insecurities about who she was and what she could achieve.

Fear is a smoke screen hiding our truth. I'm sure you have heard that the acronym F.E.A.R. stands for False Evidence Appearing Real. Fear is like a smoke screen that appears before us with an image that looks so real, like a mirage in the desert. It seems that all around us we see the evidence that what we perceive as reality is indeed the truth. So, it becomes established in our hearts. It becomes one of those squatters on our land.

Fear is always based on the future. We imagine what is going to happen or what might happen if we try something or venture out in a direction toward our dreams. I found that our greatest fears are directly connected to our deepest passions and highest calling. The things that we are uniquely designed to do, our purpose and passion in this life, seem too big and impossible because of our greatest fears.

These fear messages are whispered to our hearts from our inner critic who tells us that we are not good enough, smart enough, educated enough, experienced enough, old enough, young enough, or some other form of "not enough," and the fear that we will fail or lose in some way becomes a huge brick wall stopping us in our tracks.

That's what was happening to Marguerite. It happened to me, too. As an elementary school teacher, I felt passionate about helping the students who struggled the most. For years, I wanted to go back to school and get a master's in special education, but fear stopped me.

"You don't have what it takes. You're going to fail. You're just not good enough."

Those were the words spoken to me on my very first day as a student-teacher. It was my last semester of college and my first student teaching assignment. If I didn't do well, I likely wouldn't graduate.

For as long as I can remember, I wanted to be a teacher. As a child, most of my play revolved around teaching and playing school. I played school all the time, with anything and everything I could get my hands on.

My Barbie dolls were always in school. I had little cartoon characters called Tiny Kens that were consistently placed in neat little rows with a teacher in the front of the room. I would play for hours with them. I invited the neighborhood kids to my house and we would play school. I would try to teach them something that they didn't already know. All I wanted to do was teach. That was my passion.

And here I was finally standing in front of a roomful of fresh-faced fifth graders sitting in neat little rows eagerly awaiting my instruction. It should have been the best day of my life, but instead it was one of the worst. I stood there. The silence was deafening. Everyone was waiting for me to speak. The pressure was intense.

But I couldn't. I completely froze, terrified. My mind was a total blank. The blood drained from my head, and my heart pounded wildly in my chest. I felt like I would faint any moment. I wanted to disappear.

I bombed. I failed. I crashed and burned. My supervising teacher took over the lesson. Later, she pulled me aside to give me her feedback.

She said, "You're not going to make it as a teacher. You don't have what it takes. You're going to fail."

Those words took root in the soil of my heart and became one of those squatters.

I did graduate with my teaching degree, and I taught elementary school for years. But I stayed in small schools and small classrooms because I believed I didn't have what it took to teach in public schools with larger classrooms. I always wanted to get a master's degree in education, but I never went for it because I didn't think I had what it took.

Fast forward to my mid-fifties, I experienced a strong desire to teach in community college, helping adults who struggled with learning disabilities to prepare for college. However, I didn't have that master's degree, so I couldn't pursue that passion. I had allowed that fear years ago to become an obstacle to something I was uniquely designed to do, and it had limited my options.

This was during my stirring-up phase, my awakening, and although I couldn't pursue that specific path, I was determined that fear would not stop me from finding another way to use my gifts to help others develop their potential. I decided to dig deep and get to the root of all that fear. Once I did that, I was able to get out my megaphone and declare with authority and power that those fears had to go.

Love wipes fear out. The first step to busting through the fear and not letting it stop you is to realize that your fears are based on something that hasn't happened yet, so they're not real. You are projecting into the future and imagining what might happen rather than living in the present moment and focusing on what you want to create and bring into your life as you move along your path. It is like watching a weather forecast and then canceling your plans for a hike because the forecast said there is a 20 or 30 percent chance of rain. The sun is shining and there's not a cloud in the sky, but you cancel the fun outing because it might rain.

Marguerite was canceling her chances of learning new things because of the forecast in her mind that she might fail. Did she struggle with learning in school? Yes, she did. Had it rained before? Yes, it had. But it was not raining now, and Marguerite was not failing now. In fact, she was a successful leader already, but she didn't see herself that way because her focus was on that forecast of failure rather than the sun of success shining in her life.

We worked on changing the narrative in her mind, the forecast story, from focusing on what could go wrong to focusing on what could go right. She needed to change the narrative in her mind from that fear-based story of what could happen to a faith-based statement of what she wanted to happen. That enabled her to create actionable goals and steps to get her moving forward.

This is a switch in your thoughts from fear to love. Why? Because fear involves some sort of punishment. Fear thoughts are based on the belief that you're going to lose or suffer in some way. The Bible declares that perfect love casts out all fear (1 John 4:18). How does that work?

Research in the area of neuroscience shows us that our default mindset is actually rooted in love, not fear. Fear is learned. Dr. Leaf shares this amazing discovery: "Science is, in fact, showing us there is a massive 'unlearning' of negative toxic thoughts when we operate in love. We can unlearn negative fear—it is not a part of our innate natural functioning—our Perfect You."[9]

Operating in a loving mindset is how we were wired. When we operate in fear, we're stepping out of how we were created to live. You can wipe out fearful, toxic thoughts and the emotions they create by stepping back into a loving mindset. Love does not expect punishment or things to go wrong. Love always hopes. Love always trusts. Love looks for the good. When we focus on what is wrong with us, as Marguerite used to do, our brains create toxic thinking and emotions of fear. Stress hormones are released, and our brains are bathed in them, causing us to be overwhelmed, upset, and stuck. Our thinking is foggy, and we're carried away by the emotion.

However, if we focus on what is right and good with us and know that we are loved and that there is a good plan for our lives, our brains are flooded with hormones such as dopamine and serotonin. We calm down. We can think clearly again. We can choose how we want to respond.

When I was struggling with fear about investing in a coach training program and starting a business at the age of sixty-one, I felt confused, anxious, and stressed. I was in a fear mindset and focused only on what could go wrong. When I switched my focus from what could go wrong to what could go right, it changed everything.

My fear-based thoughts went something like this: "What are you thinking? You can't spend all that money on training at your age! How will you ever pay it all back? You're too old to start a business. You don't know anything about marketing and finding clients. Why would anyone hire you anyway?" You get the picture. I was imagining myself as a failure before I started. But none of that had happened yet.

One day while working in my office in the Women's Center at Virginia Tech, these fear-based messages were swirling around in my head. Something clicked in my heart as I was mulling all this over.

I stood up, looked out the window, and said to myself (I may have said it out loud, even), "I'm alive, well, strong, and healthy! I have lots of life still to live, and I have a purpose yet to fulfill.

I get to decide what I want to do with my life while I am still breathing. I am smart, and I can learn whatever I need to learn to make this work and be successful. I am going for it!"

Can you feel the energy shift there? All those fears simply vanished. I was filled with excitement, confidence, and a strong belief in myself that propelled me into my new life as a coach. I stepped back into a loving mindset. Love for myself, love for my purpose, and trusting that the God who loved me and created me had only good things in store for me.

I have never regretted that decision for even one moment. It was a crossroads moment in my life where I had two paths in front of me. I could choose the "safe" path and continue doing what was comfortable and familiar, yet unfulfilling, or I could choose the path toward what fired me up and made me feel alive.

Look your fears square in the face and challenge them. Write out exactly what those messages are saying to you and then question the truth of them. Are they real or are they a projection into a future that has not yet happened? Then stand up and declare your truth over the estate of your life. Tell those fears to get lost and then speak love over your life. Declare what you really want to do and what direction you want to go and believe that you were meant for this. Where is your heart telling you to go? What is love saying about you?

Choose the path that follows your heart. Marguerite followed her heart. She faced her fear and challenged it by taking her first step to volunteer at a coffee shop. Even though she was afraid she would mess up something or struggle to learn how to do whatever was required, she chose to believe in herself and love herself. So, she pressed through the fear and did it anyway. Her coffee shop experience was like going back to school for her. She learned so much about herself and discovered that even though she made mistakes as she learned the job, it was okay. Her gift for connection and helping people was one of her top strengths, and as she leaned into that, her confidence increased as her light shone in that place. She encouraged people and made them laugh, and she infused joy into the place by being herself. She stepped out of fear and into love.

Her coffee shop experience proved to be a huge stepping-stone for her to go on to greater things. About a year later, she enrolled in a nine-month leadership program, which involved quite a bit of reading and learning. The year after that, she led a team on a mission trip to Costa Rica. Marguerite discovered that her fears were not real. She now has an insatiable appetite to continue her personal development and to step more into her strengths as a leader.

Remember this from Dr. Leaf the next time you experience fear: "Fear may be powerful if we give it energy through our thinking, feeling, and choosing, but it is important to remember that love is much more powerful, and our brains were made to operate in love."[10]

Shame—makes you hide. Shame and guilt often get used interchangeably, but they are different. Guilt is feeling bad about what you did, while shame is feeling bad about *who you are*. Shame is a showstopper for sure. It will keep you hiding behind the curtains of your life, trying to live from the shadow of your true self, rather than stepping fully out into the light and taking center stage, confident in who you are.

Shame goes right to your identity and makes you feel bad for being you.

"The majority of shame researchers and clinicians agree that the difference between shame and guilt is best understood as the differences between 'I am bad' and 'I did something bad.' Shame is about who we are, and guilt is about our behaviors."[11]

Miriam-Webster defines shame as a painful emotion caused by consciousness of guilt, shortcoming, or impropriety or a condition of humiliating disgrace or disrepute. Shame can also be described as an unpleasant self-conscious emotion that involves negative evaluation of the self. When people feel shame, the focus of their evaluation is on the self or identity.[12]

In the Bible, we see Adam and Eve hiding and covering themselves after they had disobeyed God and eaten from the forbidden tree. Adam said, *"I heard thy voice in the garden, and I was afraid, because I was naked; and I hid myself"* (Gen. 3:10).

That describes the feeling of shame perfectly. It's the feeling of being exposed as someone who is worthless. It is often connected with a behavior, but the underlying root of shame is the feeling that "I am worthless as a human being. There is something about who I am as a shameful person, so I must hide who I am."

In 2 Timothy 1:8, Paul is admonishing Timothy to *"be not ashamed."* That word for *ashamed* has its roots in a word that means "disfigurement and disgrace." I am disfigured. There is something inherently wrong with me as a person, either because I have done this thing or I did this thing *because* I am worthless, disfigured, and a disgrace as a human being.

That is where shame gets its real power. For me, this was the root of all that overgrowth in my garden vision. My heart was covered with shame, and underneath that shroud, I felt worthless, disfigured, and like a disgrace as a human being, and especially as a woman. It started in my youth, as a thirteen-year-old girl out in the woods with a boy behind my friend's house as he attempted to put his hands underneath my clothes. Although it didn't go any further, he told the kids at school that he had gotten to "second base" and word got back to my older brother, who then told my mom. This was his way of protecting me, but when my mom and brother confronted me, all I felt was utter shame. I even packed a suitcase, planning on running away. You see the pattern of shame? It makes you want to withdraw and run away. It makes you want to hide.

My mom was wonderful, of course. She showered me with love and acceptance, which is the very antidote to shame. She sat me down and talked with me about respecting myself and standing up against the advances of boys who wanted to take advantage of me. She encouraged me to decide that I would not give my body away to any boy or man until I was married and with someone who loved me. She wanted me to have that decision firmly settled in my heart before I was in a situation like that again. It would be easier to resist any temptation if I'd already decided to respect myself and insist on being respected by other people as well. She was so wise, and her advice and loving acceptance helped me shrug off that shame.

I was empowered by that talk with my mom to create those boundaries in my life. I was determined to hold on to my virginity until I married.

However, that is not how things worked out. One night in my sophomore year of college, my roommate and I went out to a local hangout for a fun evening. We played foosball and talked with some cute guys. The next moment I remember, I awoke in my bed with one of those guys on top of me, but I couldn't figure out what was happening. I blacked out again. When I came to in the morning, I saw blood on the sheets. That's when I knew. I had lost my virginity in a "one-night stand." Or at least, that was how my mind framed it. The devastation and shame I felt from that event went so deep, I have never been able to find the words to describe it. I had given up something so precious to some guy I had just met in a bar. How awful! Then the message came that would define me for years to come: "You are nothing but trash."

It wasn't until my mid-fifties that I realized I had been raped. All those decades, I believed it was my fault, that somehow, I had brought that on myself. I hid it as deeply as I could in my heart. I tried to bury it and never look at it again, thinking that it would go away. Of course, it didn't go away. It became embedded in my core identity and its roots went deep. The shame storm was immense, and its effect was devastating to my heart and my life, but I did not realize it.

I believed that I was used up and worthless as a woman. This caused me to be extremely vulnerable emotionally because my heart wanted to feel that I was worthy of being loved by someone—anyone. Men took advantage of that vulnerability, and in my trauma-induced fog, I didn't realize what was happening. If a man paid attention to me, I grabbed hold of that, but it only led to more exploitation.

That destructive path led me to sitting on barstools in Las Vegas casinos waiting for a "john" to come along and ask me if I was "working." So many nights I sat in those bars wondering how in the world I got there. The shame had become so thick over my heart by this point, I felt that I was trapped in that lifestyle. I didn't believe I deserved anything better.

One customer asked me why I was doing it. He said that I wasn't like the other girls. He told me that I didn't belong there— that I was better than that. I thought he was kind for saying that, but he was wrong. I deserved this. I had brought it all on myself. The shame was thick and heavy, and I saw no escape or redemption. The man who supposedly loved me would send me out to the streets again tomorrow night and the night after that and the night after that. He believed that was all I was worth.

That my body and beauty were created to be for sale and that was how I was meant to make money. If he believed that was my worth, then it must be true. This must be my lot in life. My heart could not imagine a way out, and my mind could not conceive of a plan to get out of the situation I had allowed myself to get in. I was trapped.

I only had one friend during those three miserable years. Her name was Julie, and she was also being trafficked. Her situation was worse than mine because her pimp was physically abusive. We lived in the same apartment complex and hung out by the pool during the day, pretending that our lives were normal, until night came, and we were sent back out to the casinos. We talked for hours about what life could be like if we could just get out of there and away from those men. It seemed impossible to both of us. So, we built walls around our hearts and did what we had to so that we could survive.

I still didn't realize that I was a victim. I thought it was all my fault.

In our day, when we hear so much about the Me Too movement, it is painfully obvious that my story is not unusual or rare. Unfortunately, there is an incredible number of women in our world who have been and are being exploited in this way and bearing the scars and the shame from the atrocities being committed against them. Did you know that one in four women have experienced rape or attempted rape during their lifetimes?[13]

You may be one of them. If you are, please allow my story to help you find your freedom and the way back to your true self. Whatever was done to you does not define you. That is not who you are. You may have something else in your life that has caused you to experience this shame. All of us have experienced pain and suffering in this world. It is a part of life.

When I was rescued from that pit of despair that glorious night as I prayed with my mom over the phone, I had the strength and courage to stand up for myself and refuse to be intimidated any longer. It wasn't my strength—it was God's strength in me.

But that was only the beginning of my journey to wholeness and freedom.

Things became more complicated a year later when my ex-boyfriend, who had moved to his parents' home in Pennsylvania, convinced me to marry him. My mother tried hard to talk me out of it, but the lie I believed in my heart was that no other man would marry me after what I had done, so if I ever wanted to get married, I should just go ahead and marry him. At least he knew my past—he was a part of it.

On our wedding night, I realized what a horrible mistake I had made. I felt imprisoned all over again. I've asked myself hundreds of times why I put myself back in that relationship after all he had put me through. I beat myself up over it for years. My understanding came much later during my Truth-Telling when I learned more about the effects of trauma on a person's psyche. There is a term I've learned recently called *trauma bonds*. It explains why I went back into that relationship and then stayed in a toxic marriage for another seven years.

According to an article by Shannon Wolf in *Christian Counseling Today*, a trauma bond strongly ties a victim with their abuser in "an explosive attachment wrapped with confusion and topped off with trauma and despair." Trauma bonds are formed through a cyclic process whereby the abuser "identifies and meets the needs of the victim by professing their love." Then, the abuser gains more control through the use of gaslighting, withdrawal of attention or affection, punishment, and devaluing so that the victim will do anything to get back into the abuser's good graces. Often the victim doesn't even know what they have done, or supposedly did, to merit the anger or displeasure of the abuser. This dynamic creates a powerful bond that is extremely difficult to break and "creates profound, lifelong wounds."[14]

It was vital for my healing to understand this dynamic so that I could release myself from all the blame for allowing it to happen. When you are reclaiming your heart, you need to be kind to yourself and give yourself grace. You need to understand that you are a human who makes mistakes and bad choices, just like every other human on the planet. And you must see those squatters for what they are. They are intruders that don't belong in your heart. You can clear them out and break off the shame that covers up the real you. And when you do, you will discover that you are amazing and valuable. Your true self is in there, longing to shine out its beautiful light to the world. Breaking off the shroud of shame is necessary for you to take center stage of your life and stand in your light for all the world to see.

Guilt—makes you feel weighed down. Guilt comes from feeling bad about something you've done or not done. It can become a heavy weight you carry around like a backpack full of rocks. Guilt can also work hand in hand with shame if you believe that what you did or didn't do is a result of who you are.

Many women suffer from what I call "mommy guilt." They feel guilty whenever they invest in themselves, do something just for fun, or spend money or time on themselves. Women are natural nurturers and caregivers and will usually put the needs of their families before their own. Sometimes, their needs go unmet and unfulfilled, and they become worn out and weighed down with many burdens.

Kathryn was racked by mommy guilt whenever she took any time for her creative endeavors. She is amazingly creative, with a bottomless well of ideas, books, and programs for children. As a homeschool mom of five children, she has poured her life into her family with love and passion. Her children are evidence of the amazing gifts their mother possesses. But Kathryn felt stifled. She had so much more bubbling up inside her that she yearned to create, but when she took time away from her family to focus on these ideas, even if it was just an hour, she felt so guilty, it made her feel physically sick.

The messages she heard in those moments were things like, "I am being selfish. I shouldn't be taking this time away from my family. This is time I will never get back!" As a result, she was stuck in a constant tug-of-war between her love for her family and her passionate creativity burning inside her heart.

In our work together, we had to unload that backpack of stones she was carrying around so she could be free to be who she was created to be. To do that, we began taking out those rocks one at a time and looking at the messages they carried. Where did they come from? Were they even true?

Sometimes guilt comes from something we have done, said, not done, or not said that is legitimately wrong or hurtful to others. How do we remove those rocks? It's simple. We confess and agree that we were wrong. We own it and, if possible, go back to that person to make amends and ask for forgiveness.

Often the guilt we are carrying is based on lies. This was Kathryn's problem. She didn't have anything to feel guilty about because she wasn't doing anything wrong. The guilt she carried was created by false conclusions she had established in her heart about how she should spend her time as a mother.

This went very deep for her as the seeds for this belief were sown in her heart as a child. She had developed a "time scarcity" mindset that caused her to feel horrible anytime she even thought about taking time for herself. If what she was doing was not benefitting someone else, it felt like a waste of time to her. That produced the guilt. This became a vicious cycle.

One of the roots of this belief came from her childhood. Her family moved twenty-five times before she was in college. They once lived in a house for only six weeks. She never had time to form friendships with other girls. She had to give up a lot of things because they were always moving. Kathryn felt like she had been saying goodbye all her life. When her grandfather died, there was intense grief. She remembered getting into car after car, saying goodbye repeatedly to relationships. Time with the people she loved seemed scarce.

This had created her time scarcity mindset when it came to spending time with her family. If she spent time on herself, she was wasting precious time she could be spending with her family and other people in her life. This belief became a weight of guilt and kept her from fully pursuing her personal goals and dreams.

If you are weighed down by a burden of guilt, check your heart. Explore where this guilt may have originated. Was it spurned by deeds that were hurtful to others? Or does it come from false conclusions established in your heart? It is worth the effort to do some digging here. That is often the only way to clear out the squatters.

It takes time and energy to do this work. It can be unpleasant and uncomfortable and even painful. You may be thinking that this is just too much. You don't have the time, and it feels so exhausting. I know that feeling. I lived there for decades.

It was as if I lived on the front porch of my life. My house (my inner self) was a mess, full of trash that I didn't want to face. So, I shut the door and lived on the front porch. I didn't want to let anyone inside to see the trash. I didn't want to look at it either. My life wasn't bad; it was comfortable and filled with many wonderful things. I could have chosen to stay there, but if I did, I would have confined my life to a tiny space. I would have remained living a "front-porch" existence, never knowing the depths of who I am meant to be.

It is an exquisite journey, this journey to the depths of your heart to clear out all those squatters. It will yield abundant fulfillment and overflowing joy. You only have this one life on earth. You are meant to thrive and flourish and be deeply rooted in love—the love of God for you, His unique creation. It's a pure love, an everlasting, unconditional, deeply passionate love.

And when you clear out all the junk and see yourself the way God sees you, then you can unapologetically love yourself, too. This is your gift to the world. To love yourself as you are and to become all that you are meant to be.

THREE POWERFUL RESULTS OF RECLAIMING YOUR HEART

1. You take back your power and ownership of your life. Facing your fears and realizing that they are based on false beliefs rather than truth, gives you boldness to take back the authority over your life, your thoughts, and your emotions, and you're empowered to go into action instead of shrinking back. You find your voice, and you pick up the megaphone to declare over your life that you can do what you've been created to do.

You discover that you are fully equipped with everything you need to pursue your passions and step into your true calling. You choose your destiny—you are no longer a victim to those false beliefs and fearful thoughts. This empowers and motivates you to speak over your heart how amazing you truly are and to declare into the atmosphere all that you want to manifest in your life.

When you speak from that place of love, faith, and power, you begin to see the unlimited possibilities and opportunities before you. Creative ideas begin to flow, excitement and energy are ignited in your soul, and you no longer hold back.

You take responsibility for your beliefs, thoughts, emotions, and actions. This puts you in the driver's seat of your life. The opinions of others no longer have to drive you. You can choose what you will do or won't do. You can be open to other opinions and advice without putting up walls of defense because now you know who you are and who you will become.

You are grounded and rooted in your home—your heart and core identity. This is a secure position. It's a foundation on which to build. You can open your heart to other perspectives and opinions, knowing that you can choose what is true for you and let go of what is not.

2. You know you are a unique human being who has a purpose and place in this world. Breaking off the shame that covered so much of my heart was a huge game changer for me. One day, I sat in a meeting with my pastor and my spiritual counselor. We discussed how the rape I experienced in my youth had such deep and long-term effects on my life because of the shame I had felt. My pastor said something that went straight into my heart like a laser beam of truth.

He said that I didn't know my worth and value. That event had stripped that away. This was one of those squatters on my estate, probably the main one on the porch who refused to leave.

My assignment that day was to begin to embrace the truth that I have immense worth and value in God's eyes. So much so that He died for me. My pastor asked me, "How is worth determined for something?" The worth of anything is determined by what someone is willing to pay for it. If you put something on eBay or Craigslist, for example, it is only worth what people are willing to pay. You may put a value on it of one hundred dollars, but if the highest bid is only fifty dollars, then that is its worth.

Then my pastor asked me, "What was God willing to pay for your freedom?" He paid it all. He gave the most precious gift He had—His Son, Jesus. That's how much I am worth to Him. My value in God's eyes is everything. So is yours.

Of course, I knew this in my head. I had not embraced the truth of this in my heart, so I was not free from shame. I opened my heart to receive this truth and take it as my own. It is an act of faith to do so. Your emotions will follow your beliefs. It was a choice to believe this as truth no matter what I felt or thought. I kept repeating it, speaking the words out loud and in my mind. I am worth everything. My value is equal in God's eyes to His own Son. I looked at the evidence that proves the truth of my worth and value to God. The Bible is full of this truth.

But it had to travel from my head to my heart. I literally reprogrammed my hard drive. I rewired my brain with new beliefs, which became new thought patterns. This time they were rooted in love and truth.

As I did this, the emotions followed. I pictured myself in the arms of God, being loved with an everlasting love, an unconditional love. I asked Him to make this truth real in my heart. Only God can do that. He poured His love into my innermost being. I began to feel that I was worthy of love. I began to feel my value as someone who was fearfully and wonderfully made by my Creator—wanted and cherished with a purpose and destiny in this world (Ps. 139).

The shame broke away from my heart. The shroud covering my true self lifted, and I embraced this truth. I do belong here. I am an extremely valuable and precious human being who is worthy of love, worthy of belonging, and who offers immense value to this world just by being who I am. I have a purpose and a place on this earth, and no one can stop me from fulfilling it, except me.

You also have incredible value and worth. You were created for a purpose, and your unique gifts are needed in this world. It's time to break off the shame and know that you belong. God paid the same price for your freedom, too. Whether you believe or accept that is up to you. I'm not writing this to talk you into anything. I'm simply sharing my story and my experience as it happened in my life. But know this: You are valuable, and you are worthy of belonging and being who you are. Anything that has been spoken over you or happened to you that has convinced you otherwise is a total lie. You get to choose whether to believe the lie or the truth. Shame is like a coat you choose to wear. Whatever caused you to put on that coat does not define who you are underneath. You can choose to shed that coat, and when you do, you'll see your true light shining out from within your beautiful soul.

In Chapter 6, we'll explore your inner stories and how to rewrite them so that they align with the truth of who you are. This will greatly help you to see your value and worth.

3. You are free to confidently pursue your passions without the burden of guilt. The third huge benefit of clearing out your estate is that the burden of guilt you've been lugging around will be gone. When you're no longer afraid and ashamed, you'll be able to deal with this load of guilt. Remember, we experience guilt over things we've done or have not done. This one is easier to deal with than the first two. If you have done something to hurt others or yourself, the simple solution is to forgive, but it's not always quick and easy. If you've experienced guilt based on a false conclusion, you can repent for believing that lie, forgive yourself, and then begin to establish the truth.

Because forgiveness is such a huge topic, we will explore it in depth in the next chapter.

For now, let me just say this: forgiveness is freedom for your soul. You've probably heard the saying that when you refuse to forgive, it's like drinking poison and expecting the other person to die. That is an accurate description of the effects of clinging to unforgiveness. It causes a root of bitterness to grow, and it will poison your whole being. In fact, many diseases are caused by bitterness and resentment. Have you ever been around a bitter person who refuses to let go of grudges and offenses? What does it feel like to be in the presence of that kind of energy? You come away from those interactions feeling slimed, don't you?

Forgiveness is essential, not only for your physical health but also for your mental and emotional health. Your soul needs to be free. When you forgive, you let go of the heavy load you've been carrying, and you free yourself. That's why forgiveness is necessary.

But first, spend some time with the Reclaim Your Heart exercise in your STAR Guide.

Let's go on to Chapter 5 and discover how to unchain your heart through the power of forgiveness.

Access the Digital Workbook: https://bit.ly/StarGuideWorkbook
or the Paperback Workbook: https://amzn.to/3JUkchQ

UNCHAIN YOUR HEART

*To forgive is to set a prisoner free and discover
that the prisoner was you.*

~ Lewis B. Smedes

*And be ye kind one to another, tenderhearted, forgiv-
ing one another, even as God for Christ's sake hath
forgiven you.*

~ Ephesians 4:32

FROM MY JOURNAL (AGE 51)

I dreamed that I was traveling with a group of people from place to place, and we were engaged in ministry of some kind. The problem was that I had so much luggage. I kept packing and still had more to pack. The number of bags was way too much for me to handle, and they were totally disorganized. I couldn't make sense of them. I was never ready to go when it was time to move on because my stuff was so disorganized, and it was a lot of junk that I didn't need. There were random little items everywhere that I felt I must take with me, but I couldn't figure out why. The whole situation weighed me down and stressed me out.

This was a recurring theme in my dreams. I finally decided that the message was painfully obvious. I needed to let go of all the baggage so I could move on to the next chapter in my life. I was weighed down by all of it, like chains around my feet. I couldn't move forward until I unpacked it all and let it go.

A Lesson in Forgiveness

For over thirty years, I enjoyed playing piano in church. That is an understatement. It was my all-consuming passion. I spent hours playing my piano, perfecting my techniques, and rehearsing songs until they were embedded in my heart. In time, I stepped into the role of worship leader and continued doing that for ten years. Immersing myself in music and worship leading, I grew confident in my musicianship and as a leader. It was the highlight of my week to sit down at the piano in church, place my hands on the keys, and make wonderful music with my worship team. As we lifted our voices to God, the congregation joining in, we would be transcended into a spirit-filled atmosphere as a unified body of believers. There was nothing in my life that could compare to the joy of those experiences.

In my sixth year of leading worship, I was offered the position of worship pastor at a different church than where I had been serving. This church served a local Bible college that happened to be my husband's alma mater. He wanted to start attending this church, so I accepted the position.

There were problems from the beginning. Three teams rotated on Sundays. Most of them were students at the Bible college. I was an outsider. These team members did not want me there and definitely not as their leader. I didn't understand it, but the pastor didn't seem concerned.

I led one of the teams comprised of people who lived in the community, not Bible college students. Although the atmosphere remained fairly tense, I gave my all to this church and the worship ministry. Gradually, things improved, and my team began to grow closer and create a bond. Three years in, the Bible college closed and most of the students left. That left only my team. We seemed to settle in, and things began improving.

But something was not quite right. I could feel something going on under the surface with the team, but there was nothing I could put my finger on. I talked it over with the pastor, but he dismissed my concerns and kept telling me that I was doing a wonderful job.

My confidence waned as I started second-guessing myself. At home, I agonized over arrangements of songs and spent hours trying to perfect every note I played. My husband noticed. One day as I practiced, he stopped by my piano and said, "What are you doing? Why don't you play like you used to?" I had no answer.

The feeling that I was being talked about behind my back intensified. My confidence lessened with each week that passed. I prayed for wisdom and discernment. I asked my team to bring me their concerns. I encouraged open communication. No one said a thing.

One Sunday, the worship service went exceptionally well. At least that was what I thought. The next day, my pastor asked me to come to his office. I walked into the room and knew something was wrong. The associate pastor was present, too. We sat down, and the pastor proceeded to tell me that my team members called him with a list of complaints.

I sat dumbfounded as he ran through the list. Most of their complaints were inaccurate or not true. I told the pastor that these things were just not true, but he didn't believe me.

I felt betrayed. I felt rejected. I was deeply hurt. Then came the final blow. Rather than call our team together to talk things out and bring resolution, he simply removed me from leadership. That was it. I was out. These team members were never held accountable for anything they said or for not coming to me first as their leader. The pastor did nothing to support me. My entire world crashed down around me.

I was devastated. I went home and straight to bed, curled up in a ball, and wept bitterly. My husband just held me. I didn't return to that church. Only two of the team members supported me and stood with me in my pain. I didn't hear from any of the others. This only added to my devastation.

I began attending another church where several of my close friends went. This church has a wonderful prayer and counseling ministry that helps people work through deep hurts. A few weeks after starting to attend this church, I had a meeting with the pastor to help me process what had happened.

I had just finished unloading my entire saga of disappointment and deep hurt to this pastor. In that moment, with the wounds still so raw and fresh, I expected a much different response from him than what I heard.

After telling me that I needed to forgive the people who hurt me (which I already knew I needed to do but couldn't yet go there), he said, "And you also need to repent."

Say *what*?

Did you not hear what I just told you? Did you miss the part about how the people I thought of as my friends went to my pastor to complain about me? Did you miss the part where my pastor just removed me from my leadership position without so much as a blink of an eye, where he didn't even allow me to sit down with my team and talk things out? Did you miss how faithful I had been in that position and how I had tried so hard to make everyone happy? Did you miss how devastated I feel? Did you miss that I was the one wronged here?

Those thoughts stirred up a storm of emotions about to explode out of my chest. I was dumbfounded and shocked. I came there looking for empathy, validation, and a shoulder to cry on. The only thing I managed to get out of my mouth was, "What?"

My best friend, Loretta, was there with me. I'm sure she saw the look of utter dismay and confusion on my face. She put her arm around me and patted my hand as if to say, just wait. It will all make sense soon.

That helped me calm down and breathe. I reminded myself that these two people were there for me—they were not against me—and I just needed to open my mind and heart to receive the wisdom in the room. So, that's what I did. It was the best decision I could have made. I was about to learn what forgiveness *really* means. I was about to learn the secret of real freedom.

ᴛHE Iɴᴄʀᴇᴅɪʙʟᴇ Pᴏᴡᴇʀ ᴏꜰ ᴛʀᴜᴇ Fᴏʀɢɪᴠᴇɴᴇss

Over the next two years, I experienced the power of true forgiveness. Without integrating this F-word into your language and your life, you can't truly be free.

Most people misunderstand forgiveness and hold on to their bitterness, anger, and hurt. They feel that if they forgive, then what that person did to them was okay. When we are wronged, we naturally want to be validated, and we want that person to acknowledge what they did and pay the price for it. That is a human reaction. It's normal.

Many people think that if they forgive, they will never receive the validation that they were treated badly. What they have suffered will be dismissed as if nothing happened. It makes them feel like they don't matter, and their feelings don't matter.

That was how I felt in this situation at first. I wanted—I needed—these people to own what they did, to acknowledge that they had betrayed my trust in them and our relationship. I wanted them to know how devastated I felt. I wanted them to take responsibility for their actions and their lack of integrity. I wanted them to talk to me face to face. I wanted them to pay a price for their treachery.

That didn't happen. I am the one who paid the price. I'm the one who lost my place as the leader of worship. I'm the one whose confidence was destroyed. I'm the one who felt humiliated and dismissed as if I had no value at all. They continued in their place on the worship team. They never had to face me or own up to what they did. Even now, more than sixteen years later as I write this, I have only talked to a few people on that team about what happened. Only two people reached out to me after I had been dismissed from my position, and they were the two who had not participated in the betrayal and had always been there for me. No one else from the entire church called to see how I was doing.

Imagine what shape my heart would have been in if I had not forgiven all of them over all that time. Do you know what happens to your heart when you hold on to unforgiveness? The Bible talks about a "root of bitterness that defiles many" growing inside you. It has lots of tentacles, and it reaches into every area of your life. Your body can begin to manifest disease from that bitterness, too. Have you ever known a bitter person who refuses to let go of a grudge? What kind of energy do you feel from someone like that? They often suffer from ailments such as arthritis, high blood pressure, digestion issues, heart conditions, and more. It is not worth it to hold on to unforgiveness and bitterness. It only hurts you.

Forgiveness Is About Letting Go

Those dreams told me that the load I was trying to carry with me wasn't serving me any longer. I didn't need it. It was time to let go. Forgiveness was the key to truly releasing all that baggage.

The number one thing I want you to understand is that forgiveness is for *you*, not for the person who wronged you. To forgive is to release *your heart* from the event, from the situation, from the pain and suffering. When you forgive, you cut the chains that bind you to that person and what they did. Forgiveness brings freedom.

The biblical definition of the word *forgive* means "to send forth or to give forth."[2] Rick Sizemore, the pastor who helped me learn how to forgive, always describes forgiveness as

---

[2] (Strong, *A Concise Dictionary of the Words in the Greek Testament*, n.d., 17)

the picture of flushing a load of crap down the toilet. You are sending it forth from your heart and quite literally unloading all the junk from your soul so that root of bitterness cannot grow and defile you and many others in your life.

As John Bevere said, "Bitterness is a root. If roots are nursed—watered, protected, fed, and given attention—they increase in depth and strength. If not dealt with quickly, roots are hard to pull up."[15]

Forgiveness is about letting go of the thoughts and stories you hold in your mind and heart about the person or people who wronged you. It takes a tremendous amount of energy to cling to those stories. For forgiveness to occur, you first must realize how much you are hurting yourself to hold on to the anger and resentment. When you truly forgive, it feels like a huge weight has been lifted from you, and you realize how much of a burden you've been carrying around.

Once you understand what true forgiveness is, it becomes much easier to let go of that burden. That is just the beginning of the process. Forgiveness can take time to complete, depending on the intensity of the offense and how deeply you were wounded. The first step is to choose to forgive, knowing that you are releasing the weight of it from yourself.

I started looking at each piece of baggage I was lugging around. I found I needed to forgive people from my distant past. Blanket forgiveness doesn't work. I had to unpack those bags and name specific people and specific events in this process.

This included forgiving the man who drugged and raped me when I was nineteen. I never told anyone what happened. Not a soul. I never talked about it and never received any counseling. It was the early 1970s, and no one talked about such things. If there were counselors available to me on campus, I didn't know it. And I don't think it occurred to me to seek help. I believed that I had somehow brought it on myself, so the last thing I wanted to do was tell someone what I had allowed to happen. It never dawned on me that I may have been drugged and raped. Not until one day in a freedom session in my church. I was probably fifty-six or fifty-seven. I had blamed myself for that night for over thirty-five years. That's a long time to be chained to an event!

But now the truth had been told. The lie had been uprooted from my garden. Healing could happen now. It's just like when you have an abscess or an infected wound. It can't heal until it is cleaned out. I went home that day and researched what happens when you have been given a date rape drug. I couldn't believe what I read. It was the perfect description of that night—exactly how I remembered it.

I had been taken advantage of by this person. I had unknowingly been given a drug that incapacitated me so that I no longer could make any choices about what did or did not happen with my body. I had been raped. This was not my fault. I wasn't dirty or disgusting. I was the victim, not the perpetrator.

After that freedom session, I let the floodgates open for the first time in decades. I lay on the floor and wept. I let it come, all the repressed grief, anger, and shame. It was purifying to my soul.

Releasing locked emotions helps your heart to be whole again. I didn't stuff the pain or shut down the flood of emotions this time. I let it all flow out. I was able to do so because I was fully committed to this process of healing. For the first time in over thirty-five years, I welcomed strong and painful emotions as something good, not something to be feared.

I chose to forgive the man who drugged and raped me. I didn't know his name and couldn't tell you what he looked like, but I could still go right back there into my bedroom and be on that bed with him on top of me. In this process of letting go, when I took that piece out from the baggage and looked at it, I resisted the urge to stuff it down once again. I looked at it. I faced the reality that it had indeed occurred. I went through the steps of forgiveness that I am about to share with you, and at the end of it, that piece of baggage from my past was released. It still happened. It's still a part of my story. I can still remember it. The difference is that it has no hold on me, and it has no power over me any longer.

The same is true for the man who put me out on the streets of Vegas as a prostitute. I looked at the specific events and words from those years that came up from my heart, and I dealt with each one separately through this process.

I did the same thing for myself. This was probably the hardest one. Forgiving myself—for believing that it was my fault I was drugged and raped, for allowing myself to be exploited, for being compliant and doing something that went against everything I believed in, and for carrying the shame for all those years. Throughout this process, I wept, I struggled, I resisted at times, but I kept going. I wanted to be free of all that junk. I wanted freedom and peace. And that's what I got.

I'm going to walk you through the 7-Step Forgiveness Process that brought me freedom and peace. I'll illustrate the process using the church situation, but this is the process I used for all the baggage I needed to release from my past. I use this process anytime I need to forgive and let go.

The 7-Step Forgiveness Process

I have developed a 7-Step Forgiveness Process based on my experience and what I have learned about the power of true forgiveness. You'll find it in the STAR Guide that accompanies this book. For now, I'm going to walk you through the process as I experienced it in the situation with my worship team.

These steps don't necessarily have to be followed in the sequence I have laid out here. Often, you'll find this is a circular path or that it intertwines and doubles back, repeating itself. Sometimes you'll experience several of these steps happening at the same time. This process is not meant to be a formula, but rather a process with key elements that, when integrated, will bring you wholeness and freedom.

Step One: Acknowledge What Happened

In this first step, the goal is to talk about what happened. Get it all out, let your emotions be whatever they are, and go over all the details of what occurred. Being in a safe space with people who listen deeply without judgment is imperative. You can do this alone, but if the event was deeply wounding, I don't recommend it. I also urge you to find the right people to walk through this with you. If you talk it out with another injured soul carrying unforgiveness in their heart, you could end up in a worse place than when you started.

The purpose of this first step is not to stir up more bitterness or to cast blame and judgment on the offending party. The purpose is to unload it from your heart and mind. To acknowledge what happened brings it out into the open, and you look at the facts. It happened. You didn't make it up or imagine it.

Sometimes we don't want to talk about things that happened to us because we want to avoid the pain. This doesn't work because the memory and the hurt get lodged in your body and your heart. It doesn't go away until you get it out of yourself. Sometimes it feels wrong to talk about it because then we feel like we are complaining or judging, and that can add guilt onto our already heavy burden.

This first step is not about gossiping or complaining about the person who hurt you. Approach it as if you are an objective observer reporting the facts, like at the scene of a crime when the police question witnesses. Talk about the facts of what happened as you witnessed it. Get into the details. Get it all out.

As I sat with my friend and my pastor, I shared all the details, even the background history of this team and all that had been going on over the time period that I had been the worship leader. It was all important because it helped my heart unload all that I had been sensing and feeling. I shared things that had been spoken to me over the years in that church. I talked about how I felt that there was something wrong but couldn't uncover the root of it. I shared all the details about the meeting with my pastor and what he relayed to me regarding what the others had told him about my leadership skills or the lack of them. I shared how the pastor decided simply to remove me from the position without allowing me to meet with the team to talk this all out.

My new pastor and my friend gave me the space to talk. They listened without interruption. It felt amazing to have that space and to be listened to in such a deep, compassionate manner.

Step Two: Validate Your Emotions

I was angry, mostly. That anger was my default armor that covered up the deeper emotions. I also felt betrayed and rejected. I was deeply hurt. I felt like a failure, and shame accompanied that one. All those emotions needed to be acknowledged and validated before I could move through this process of total forgiveness. I tend to disconnect from my emotions and stuff them or mask them with anger. This has been my pattern all my life, but it became even more embedded into me after experiencing all the sexual trauma of my early adult years. I mastered it. It wasn't that I just hid my emotions. I didn't feel them. I numbed.

In this event, though, I felt the anger and the deep hurt of betrayal and rejection. I didn't know what to do with those emotions, and I even felt guilty for having them. As a good Christian, I should not be feeling this way toward others. In addition, I like to maintain an inner peace and calm, which is a major trait of my personality type. So, feeling all these strong emotions was upsetting that inner calm.

When you are walking through this forgiveness process, this step is incredibly important. We tend to judge ourselves for the emotions we are experiencing. We think we shouldn't be feeling them, and we often apologize for what we feel, or we are ashamed that we feel the way we do. But emotions are not good or bad or right or wrong. You are human. Humans experience emotions.

Think of emotions as signposts or signals. They show you what is happening within you. Accept your emotions just as they are. Allowing yourself to feel them is healthy and will help you process the event and heal from it instead of holding on to it. It helps me to picture these emotions as waves crashing on the shore and then ebbing away.

Allowing emotions to crash and ebb through my soul and my body has been so important. I have learned that it is a choice, though. At first, I needed to become aware of my subconscious habit of avoiding feeling anything. When I first became aware of my tendency to numb my emotions, I was astounded. I remember watching a movie once where someone was suffering a tragedy. I felt compassion and sadness well up inside, tears formed in my eyes, and then, just like that, a wall of numbness shut it all down. Once again, I felt nothing. That was the first time I watched it happen, and I couldn't stop it.

Since then, I have learned to relax, let go of the fear of experiencing strong emotion, and give myself permission to be open and vulnerable. I had to stop the wall from coming down and tell myself that it was okay to feel again. When I sat by my mom's deathbed and said goodbye, I was keenly aware of the crashing waves of grief and sadness inside, and I gave them permission to come in their full intensity. It was a very healing experience.

Just as a cleanse might clear out the toxins that accumulate in your body, it's equally important to your overall wellbeing to release the toxic effects of emotions that have been stuck in your mind, heart, and soul. It's like unclogging a well or a pipe so the water can flow pure and clear again. The deep fountain of your soul and spirit is life-giving, and when it is clogged up with unreleased and unprocessed emotions and memories, unforgiveness, and unhealed hurts, you can't access that flow of energy. It's poisoning your system.

These stuck emotions affect your body as well. Many diseases stem from unprocessed trauma and other events that create stress in our bodies. Studies have found many health problems related to stress. Stress seems to worsen or increase the risk of conditions like obesity, heart disease, Alzheimer's disease, diabetes, headaches, depression, anxiety, gastrointestinal problems, asthma, accelerated aging, and even death. This is because when you're stressed out, your body produces higher levels of cortisol, sometimes known as the "stress hormone."[16]

All emotions need to flow through the body. Emotions are energy, and when they are not released, when we hold on to them, they get stuck in our bodies as well as our souls. Think of the word *emotion* as two parts: E-motion or "energy in motion."

Realizing that no emotion is inherently good or bad goes a long way toward helping you unlock these stuck emotions. Often, we try to avoid feeling an emotion because we think we shouldn't be feeling it, and we beat ourselves up over the fact that we are feeling what we're feeling. In my case, I didn't like experiencing deep, painful emotions, so I avoided feeling anything at all. But that was a judgment I was making about painful emotions—that they are bad, and I shouldn't experience them.

One thing that we have learned from the field of neuroscience is that emotions are not things that happen to us. Emotions are created by us. They are created in our brains, and often we are not aware of that fact. We feel physical pain or other sensations because emotions show up in our bodies.

"Emotions aren't your reactions to what situations mean; they are what situations mean. Emotions don't cause you to act in any way. They are an indication of how you are understanding what's happening in your own body in relation to what's going on around you in the world."[17]

Understanding our emotions, where they come from, and what they can teach us is a huge step toward healing and wholeness. It takes patience, guidance, and support to sit with strong emotions. It takes courage and commitment. It takes getting out of our heads and into our hearts. When we are willing to slow down and allow ourselves to be more self-aware, tuning in to what our heart and body tell us, we're then able to dislodge stuck emotions. This is a very restorative process. It is a process that should become a practice in your life, not a one-time event.

My pastor and my friend allowed me to express my anger and hurt that day, without judgment. They encouraged me to let those emotions be what they were. They validated them by recognizing that it was completely understandable that I would feel all those emotions given what had happened. Of course, I would feel angry, hurt, betrayed, and rejected by the people I had trusted when they complained about me to the pastor. Of course, I felt like a failure when my pastor removed me from leadership. Those emotions are normal and make sense in that situation. Anyone would feel that way. It did happen. They were wrong in how they handled the situation. Saying that and putting it out on the table as fact enabled me to feel supported, heard, and understood.

Now, I could breathe and open my heart to move to the next step. That's what validating your emotions does for you. Let them all come out, crash on the shore, and then let them ebb away naturally.

This next step took me totally by surprise.

STEP THREE: TAKE RESPONSIBILITY FOR YOUR RESPONSE

If you're a Christian, I would say that this is the step where you repent. When my new pastor said this to me that day, my jaw must have hit the floor.

He gently explained the two sides to forgiveness. Imagine you have a ball and chain attached to both of your feet. One of them has to do with holding on to unforgiveness toward that person or people. When you forgive them, you are released from only one chain. If you don't deal with the other one, you will remain tied to that event, and you'll continually experience those overwhelming emotions. You won't be free from the whole situation. This is the reason most people struggle with feeling like they haven't forgiven even when they have tried to forgive.

The second chain has to do with my response to what happened. Did I complain and judge these people? Did I hold on to resentment and bitterness toward them? Did I feel hatred toward them and want them to feel hurt, too? Did I see them as bad people? Was I holding on to my anger as a weapon against them?

I had to admit that all of these were true. Although they are completely natural reactions and emotions to feel, I began to see that I was choosing to hold on to them, and if I was being honest with myself, I had to admit that I was treating them the same way they had treated me. It is natural for us to want to retaliate when we have been wronged. We all want to see that person pay for what they did to us. The problem is that when we respond that way and hold on to those thoughts and emotions, we harm ourselves. It is like drinking poison and expecting them to die. We are keeping ourselves chained to the event, and it causes bitterness to become rooted in our hearts.

My pastor asked me to repent for complaining and holding on to anger, bitterness, hatred, and judgment toward all these people. *Repent* means simply to change your mind. It means that you change the agreements you've established in your heart. I needed to stop agreeing that they were horrible, evil people and agree that they were humans with faults and imperfections, just like me. I began to see them not as monsters, but as human beings. I needed to agree that I was also imperfect.

Slowly, over time, I worked through all of these, but this didn't completely resolve itself in that one session that day. It took time. I went through this process repeatedly for the next year until I felt a complete release from all of it. I knew I was free when I could think about each person involved and feel nothing but peace and love in my heart. When I could genuinely wish them well and pray blessings over their lives and feel love for them, then I knew I was free.

This step is difficult for many people for one understandable reason. It feels like you're letting them off the hook. It feels like you're saying that what they did was okay, and they can go on their merry way without any repercussions. It may feel that way, but that is not at all what this is about. This is about releasing you from the burden of carrying around this event in your heart. When you see this person, or in my case, people, through the lens of what they did to you and that's all you can see, you are sitting in judgment of them. That's not a safe place to be. We are not their judge. Only God has that position. When you let go of the anger, hatred, bitterness, complaining, and judgment, you step out of the way and give God room to move in the situation. And He will. God judges and convicts people of their sin. We can't know the motivations of their hearts. We can discern the fruit of their lives, such as their words and actions, and use wisdom to navigate our relationship with them. But when we stand in a place of judgment on them as a person, we bring on ourselves the same measure of judgment we are giving them. This will not bring you peace or freedom.

One way to let go of judgment and unforgiveness is to do a little role-play exercise. Do this somewhere completely private if possible. Place a chair in front of you and imagine that the person who wronged you is sitting in that chair facing you. Talk to them, out loud, and say everything you want to say to them. Express your emotions fully. Tell them how they hurt you. Let it all out. Shout, scream, and cry if you need to. Once you have emptied yourself of all your emotions, sit quietly for a moment, looking at this person. Imagine them speaking to you now. Let them tell you all you need to hear from them. Let them tell you how sorry they are about what they've done and how they hurt you. Hear their heart and the struggles they are walking through. Allow your heart to empathize with them. See them as human beings with weaknesses and faults just like you. Allow compassion to rise in your heart toward them.

Now it's your turn to talk to them again. This time, you will speak blessings over them. Pray for God to bless their life and heal their heart. As you do this, you may sense a swell of love and compassion for this person. I know that seems strange, and it may feel strange, too. After all, this person has been your enemy. But let that love and compassion flow out of your heart and through your words. Pour it out in abundance. This is true freedom. When you can pray for your enemies and bless them from your heart, no part of the past hurt from this person can touch you or hurt you.

After I had taken responsibility for the way I responded and all the bitterness I had carried in my heart toward them, that second ball and chain was released from my heart. This made it much easier to empathize and have compassion for them.

I did this exercise, imagining my former pastor sitting in that chair. By the end of it, I was so filled with love for this man. I saw him as a man who lived with so much pressure and many fears. My anger and bitterness toward him for not supporting me and not standing up for me as one of his staff members through that entire situation totally dissipated. My heart was released from the burden of carrying around that offense. I sincerely wanted him to be blessed, to prosper, and to be happy. I felt so light.

STEP FOUR: FORGIVE

If you have thoroughly walked through steps one through three, this step is the easiest thing to do. You simply forgive. Speak it out loud: "I forgive, (name the person), for (name the specific event and how it made you feel). I forgive (name) and release them completely."

That's it! Now, check your heart. Think about the event and the person, and see what emotion comes up. Do you still feel a stab in the gut? Do you still feel anger boiling up? Do you still feel like they should pay for what they did? If you do, you're not done yet. Go back through the steps and continue doing so until you can forgive freely and without any attachment to what happened. Give it time.

Step Five: Address Your Unmet Needs

In step five, you spend time expressing those things that were left unsaid and acknowledge the needs that were unmet or ignored. This is where you practice self-compassion and self-love. We've spent a good amount of time on what happened, but what about what *didn't* happen? Sometimes that is just as important to address and acknowledge for your heart to be completely healed and whole again.

For me, those things deeply affected my confidence and my worth and value, not only as a worship leader but as a person who wanted to be appreciated and honored, to belong and to be loved, like anyone else on the planet. If you have ever experienced the pain of a friend's betrayal, going behind your back to talk about you to someone else, then you know the devastation that can do to your heart. You feel so dishonored and rejected like you're not worth someone's time and respect. It literally can feel like a stab in the back and it's humiliating.

Even after I did the first four steps and felt that I had completely forgiven the pastor and the members of the worship team, my heart and my confidence were still clearly damaged. Before all this happened, I used to sit at the piano and play for hours on end, immersed in the music and caught up in worship. It was the passion of my heart and I loved it. But after this experience, I found myself avoiding the piano. When I did sit down to play, I couldn't push past all the condemning thoughts bombarding my mind. Thoughts like, "You can't play the piano. You suck! How could you have ever thought you were any good at this?" The joy and passion were gone—I only heard the words of my critics, constantly mocking me and telling me what a failure I was as a musician and as a leader.

I didn't touch my piano for a year.

My heart had been crushed, and any confidence I had was squashed under the feet of those critical words. Needs and wants had to be addressed and expressed for me to heal and move forward.

I needed to hear that I was in no way a failure. I needed to know that my ten years as a worship leader had meant something, that my ministry had blessed others, and that I was a good musician. I needed to be acknowledged for my faithfulness as a leader, for the service I had given to my church and my team. I wanted to hear that I had done a good job and that I had been a valuable part of that church's mission.

So, I wrote all these needs and wants out in my journal. I spent time in meditation, prayer, and reading the Bible to know and be assured of God's tender love for me. I needed to hear His thoughts toward me. As I poured out my heart in the pages of my journal, from the depths of my spirit, I heard the whispers of God's heart infusing into my being that I am worthy of love, that I have great value in His eyes, and that He was pleased with my faithful service as a worship leader. My journals are filled with His delight and pleasure in my worship of Him and my service to the church, leading others into His presence.

This step cannot be overemphasized. Express your heart's needs and ask for God's love to be poured into the empty places. If you don't believe in God, you can still open your heart to receive love from the people in your life. You can open your heart to the presence of love in the universe and all around you. I also received tons of love from my husband, family, and friends who loved me and had been blessed by my leadership in worship. As you open your heart and ask for what you need, you will find many gifts of healing coming your way.

About a year and a half into this process, I ran into a friend at the post office. He gently asked me if I was aware that my former pastor was coming to speak at our church this Sunday. I felt like I had been punched in the gut. My immediate reaction was the thought, "No! He can't come to my church and hurt them, too!" I needed to release more in my heart. I was not completely free. I was so surprised because I thought I was done with it.

I went home and walked through this forgiveness process once more. I forgave him again. I searched my heart for the remaining anger, bitterness, hatred, and judgment that I stuffed into the crevices of my heart. I let it all go and blessed him again. At some point during this session, a thought popped into my consciousness, ever so softly. It came in the form of this prayer: "Lord, I know that I need to forgive him even though he has never acknowledged what he did. And I do forgive him, but it would be so nice if he told me that he was sorry for how he handled the situation. It would be so nice if he admitted that he had been wrong and that I had been treated unfairly." It was a quick thought and then it was gone. But my heart had just revealed something I desperately needed.

A few days later, the unthinkable happened. I was shopping at Walmart, walking through the sock department, when I saw him talking on his cell phone. Our eyes made contact, and I waved but kept walking because he was on the phone.

He quickly hung up the phone and called out to me. He looked me in the eyes and asked me to forgive him for how he had treated me. He told me that he had been wrong not to stand by me and that he had let the opinion of others sway his decision. He said that he had not honored me for my faithful service to that church and that he was so sorry that he hurt me. I stood there in shock. I couldn't believe this was happening. His words felt like music to my ears, like a healing balm to my heart. I had already forgiven him without expecting him ever to acknowledge what he had done. This was like an extra special gift sent straight from heaven to my heart. It was exactly what I needed to hear.

I asked him to forgive me, too, for holding on to anger, bitterness, and resentment toward him. We had the most amazing, empowering, validating, and encouraging conversation I could ever ask for in those few minutes, standing in the sock department of Walmart!

That Sunday, he spoke at my new church. I received his message and ministry with an open and free heart. Since then, I have not had any residual resentment left in my heart toward him or any of the others on that worship team. When I think about them, I feel only love for them. I am completely and totally free!

Step Six: Uncover False Beliefs

Now you must address the false narratives you believed as a result of what happened. You've already been doing a lot of this throughout this book, but it shows up again when you go through the forgiveness process because if you don't, you'll remain tied to the event. For example, one day I was trying to play the piano but was clearly just slogging through it. My husband stopped and said to me, "I miss hearing you play the way *you* play!"

The problem was that I no longer believed I could play. I believed that I had never had any ability to play and that I had never been called to lead worship. I had allowed that lie to settle, and now it was severing me from the talent I had. I couldn't connect to it anymore. I couldn't connect to that heart of worship that had naturally flowed out through me for the previous ten years as a worship leader.

I worked on this step for an exceptionally long time. Many people poured into me during this time, often without knowing it. People would randomly tell me how much they missed hearing me play and how much they loved it when I led worship. This happened repeatedly. I believe God sent them to me because He knew I needed to hear it. I worked at recognizing my beliefs as false, reminding myself of all the wonderful times of worship I had led in the past, evidenced by what these people said to me.

My confidence slowly returned. I started playing piano again, and I eventually joined my new church's worship team. I'm not going to say that this healing process was quick. However, I decided to look at it as an opportunity to grow as a musician. I was at a place where I could listen to the criticisms of my former worship team with an open mind and heart. The offense was gone, so now I could be an objective observer and find the gifts that were there. They had some valid points. I had a lot of room to improve my skills. I began to work on those areas, and I became a better musician.

Another blessing that emerged from all that pain was a new perspective about who I am, apart from what I do. I realized that my identity had become intertwined with what I did, and not with who I am. I used to feel so out of place if I wasn't on stage playing piano and leading worship, as if that determined who I was, and without that, I felt at sea, lost and without bearings. As my heart healed, I began to see that who I am never changes. It doesn't have anything to do with my position or how I expressed my gifts. No matter what, I am a child of God, and I am loved and accepted as I am.

Over time, I began to settle into that knowledge, and an incredible peace filled my soul. I could relax and be present, enjoying the music no matter who played. I stopped comparing myself to other pianists and began to appreciate their gifts and their style. I finally embraced my unique style and stopped trying to play to please others. I only played to please God. This was an immense gift that I don't think I would have received had I not been through that painful experience. It became a precious gift to my heart.

Look at the lies that were implanted in your heart as a result of what happened. What have you started to believe about yourself? Have you started to agree with what others said about you or with what you've assumed they thought about you? We often make up stories about the intentions of others for the part they played in the situation. For example, I believed that my team members not only thought I was a terrible musician and leader, but that they didn't like me at all and were happy to be rid of me. These beliefs only intensified my thoughts about myself as a failure, but I couldn't possibly know if they were the truth.

It is important to isolate the thoughts that roll through your mind when you try to move forward but find you can't. It could be that a lie has tripped you up and is holding you hostage. But no worries. You have the power to believe whatever you want to believe. You get to choose *not* to believe the lie.

The most powerful thing you can do is to name it—write out that false belief exactly how it comes to you. How true is it really? What evidence is there to back it up? What is the origin of that thought? Then, call it a lie. I've been known to shout it out loud and say, "You're a big fat liar!" It may sound strange, but it feels very empowering to do that. It removes the power of it because you get it out of your head and separate it from you. That lie is not who you are. It is not your identity. It is just a false message you've agreed with, but now you can break that agreement and break the hold it has over you.

STEP SEVEN: ESTABLISH THE TRUTH AND RECEIVE HEALING IN YOUR HEART

Once you identify the lies and eradicate them from your life, you need to establish truth as a firm foundation so you can thrive and flourish. The truth is often the opposite of the lie. For me, in this story, my truth was not that I was a highly skilled and accomplished musician who could play at Carnegie Hall. Not even that I was ready to record and go on tour or even that I was the best worship leader in my town. That wasn't true, and I didn't need it to be true. Your truth needs to be backed by evidence that you can hook your heart into because if you don't believe it, you won't be able to establish it as a rock-solid foundation.

My truth was that I had been an authentic worshiper of God, who was passionate about being in His presence and drawing as many people into that sacred place as possible. I did this by opening my heart and soul to the Lord and playing my piano to the best of my ability. It was not playing to the utmost perfection of musicianship. It was to the best of *my* ability and in my own style.

My truth was that I had been faithful to prepare, to pray over every song list, to pour into my team, to show up fully engaged as I led worship, and to be authentic and genuine before the congregation and God. And I did that for the ten-plus years that I was a worship leader. I had fully embraced and obeyed the call with all my heart, even though I was not a highly trained musician and even though I did not have a music degree.

The truth is that God was pleased with me, and many people had been blessed through my obedience to serve. I had lots of evidence to back this truth, and as I declared it over my heart in the weeks and months following my healing, it became my solid rock. I could rest knowing that I had done well. Now I could move on to whatever the future held for me, in peace and confidence.

That is what truth will do for you. Knowing the truth makes you free.

And when you're in this space, you are positioned to allow your heart to heal.

What Does a Healed Heart Look Like?

When your heart is healed, you will be able to experience the intensity of anger or grief, hurt, and disappointment without getting stuck in a downward spiral or holding on to the emotions for too long. You can be with these emotions, feel them fully, but then allow them to be transformed into feelings of strength, power, and passion. The feeling of needing outward retaliation or revenge fades, and you no longer feel like a victim or the need to blame. Instead, you're filled with a sense of personal integrity and confidence in your ability to stand up for yourself and speak your truth with compassion and kindness for yourself and others.

This is what a healed heart looks like. It is a free heart. It is a heart filled with truth. It is a heart at peace with itself and with the world. It is a heart that knows it's worth and value and can be open, vulnerable, present, alive, hopeful, and content. This is a place of deep contentment and joy.

This process may take time. You may find that you are working in these steps simultaneously or that you stay in one for an extended period. That is fine. There is no right or wrong way to go through this process of forgiveness. In some instances, it will be quick. In others, especially for situations of deep hurt, traumatic events, and repeat offenses, it may take longer to feel released and at peace. Stick with it. Don't hold on to unforgiveness, bitterness, anger, and resentment. It only poisons your soul.

In the **STAR Guide**, you'll find the **7-Step Forgiveness Process Template** that you can use for events that you need to let go of so you can find freedom. You may find that you need to print multiple copies of this template to use with multiple events. We all have them, so there is no shame in using this process repeatedly. I urge you to do so. Forgiveness is probably the most powerful path to personal freedom that exists in this life. It is a process I still use whenever I feel wronged, mistreated, or offended. It keeps my heart free from all those chains.

Forgiveness is at the heart of living a life of love. Love for yourself and for others. The Bible tells us that *"(charity) doth not behave itself unseemly, seeketh not her own, is not easily provoked, thinketh no evil"* (1 Corinthians 13:5). When you don't hold on to wrongs you've suffered, your heart is free to love and to live.

If you would like assistance with this process and would like to pursue working with me as your coach, please visit my website and fill out the coach request form. I would be honored to speak with you and see what we can do together to help you find the freedom and peace that you deserve. Scan the QR code below to watch a special message on forgiveness.

Scan the QR Code above with your smartphone to view my special message about Forgiveness. Or, follow this link:
https://youtu.be/imQsZ5_kb64

Access the Digital Workbook: https://bit.ly/StarGuideWorkbook or the Paperback Workbook: https://amzn.to/3JUkchQ

CHAPTER 6

THE TRIALS OF YOUR HEART

The past will be your teacher if you learn from it; your master if you live in it.

~ Steve Maraboli

Therefore, behold, I will allure her, and bring her into the wilderness, and speak comfortably unto her. And I will give her her vineyards from thence, and the valley of Achor for a door of hope: and she shall sing there, as in the days of her youth, and as in the day when she came up out of the land of Egypt.

~ Hosea 2:1415

FROM MY JOURNAL (AGE 51)

(This was a word spoken to me on my first Sunday at my new church following the event I shared in the previous chapter.)

The minister said, "Hosea 2:14 says, 'I will allure her into the desert.' Don't complain—God's got you there. It's a dry time, an uncertain time, but He's got you there. God said, I will speak tenderly to her— you're expecting some kind of anger or judgment there, but the Lord said, 'I'm going to speak tenderly to her. I will give her back her vineyards, her fruitfulness again and make the Valley of Achor a door of hope.' God loves to take troubled times and open a door of hope.

"The door was being opened to a much greater freedom than you have ever imagined, to explore limits that were clearly upon you or were out of your reach previously. God is going to open a whole new paradigm of possibility to you."

Coming Up from the Wilderness

One of my favorite verses in the Bible displays a powerful and poignant reality of a woman who's entire being has been changed through her struggles. It is found in Song of Solomon 8:5, and it says, "Who *is* this that cometh up from the wilderness, leaning upon her beloved?"

The Song of Solomon carries a twofold message. One side is about the human love relationship in a marriage. The other side is a metaphorical view of our relationship with God, the Lover of our souls. Throughout the book, this woman endures a series of experiences that lead her to a place of total acceptance and being completely loved. There are points along her journey where she feels totally alone, abandoned by her lover, and unsure of her identity. She suffers through the torment of separation from the one she loves. She endures the wounding and taunting of people around her, taking advantage of her vulnerable state and leaving her injured on the side of the road. She eventually finds the one whom her soul loves, and they are reunited. In the verse above, we see her emerging from her wilderness season, leaning on her beloved. She has pursued and found her dream, and she has been transformed in the process.

To me, this is a compelling parallel to every person's life on this earth. We are all searching for unconditional love—to be accepted, seen, known, and deeply loved for who we are. We all experience the torment of rejection and abandonment at some point in our lives. It is unavoidably part of the human experience on earth. The wounds that our hearts receive from those experiences often go very deep. Many people never recover from them and end up living a life of bitterness and resentment. They remain in bondage to their past because they refuse to receive the lessons their pain and suffering have for them.

No one enjoys suffering. At least no one I have ever met. It is natural to try to avoid pain. When trials come our way, most of us either try to run from it or get through it any way we can. Then, we try to forget about it and move on. Many of those experiences have brought shame upon us. We want to stuff that away somewhere in the dark recesses of our hearts and pretend it never happened. At least, that has been my default response.

The wilderness represents those desert seasons in our lives when it seems like nothing is happening and all seems lost. We feel isolated and forgotten. We can't see the fruit from our efforts, and we feel dry and barren inside. We're still waiting for our ship to come in. Waiting for something good to finally happen. Waiting for our circumstances to change for the better. Waiting for someone to rescue us. Waiting, waiting, waiting!

Have you ever experienced a time in your life when it seemed like you lost everything? The people you had grown close to and relied on for support abandoned you. Your title or position in your work was stripped away—maybe through being laid off or your company downsized. Your marriage ended. Someone close to you passed. You relocated to another town or city and familiar surroundings vanished. Through illness or injury, perhaps now you could no longer do the things you once enjoyed. Everything that propped up your life fell away, and you are totally on your own.

This Is the Wilderness

Most of us endure those times of waiting until something changes, like sitting in the waiting room at the doctor's office, trying to pass the time looking through a magazine or checking out what's happening on Facebook or Instagram on your phone. The waiting time seems endless.

These seasons come and go throughout our lives. The only thing constant in life is change. We know that if we hang in there long enough, eventually something will change. Then we can move on from the wilderness into the next season.

I have a different perspective now. I am like that woman stepping out of the wilderness, leaning on her beloved. I tried to endure the wilderness seasons as best I could until things changed, then I could move on. But now I see all those seasons in a new light.

What if those seasons came into your life to teach you something? What if there are gems and treasures within those experiences meant for your growth and development into your absolute best self?

I've discovered that the most significant growth and change happen through struggle. Even physically, you can't develop your muscles and sculpt your body without the pain and struggle of resistance training and lifting weights. It is impossible to build muscle tone and strength without pain. No pain, no gain! When you are working your muscles, you are causing small tears in the muscle tissue, which then heal and create stronger muscles.

Rick Sizemore says this about the benefits of enduring the trials in the wilderness: "When we have come through the trials of the wilderness, our hearts are known and safe. We know what it takes to stand in tough times. We have been proven, and now we can be trusted with the wealth and treasures of God."[18]

This same principle applies to our personal growth and development as people. We are born with amazing potential inside to be who we were designed to be, but we need to develop that potential by growing those seeds planted in our DNA. I believe that every person was uniquely designed to be and do something unlike any other person ever born. And yet, so many people allow that potential to lie underdeveloped. Many will die with their unique song still inside them.

My thought is that some people are not willing to pay the price of developing their potential. It's hard work, and it takes persistence and the willingness to suffer pain and loss. Another reason is that many people never learn the lessons from the wilderness. They haven't mined for the gold, for the treasure that exists within those desert seasons they endured in their lives.

"An empowered perspective helps me see that I can only get stronger when working against resistance. It is when I struggle that I strengthen. It is when challenged to my core that I learn the depth of who I am. It is when we feel broken that we can become experts at mending."[19]

It's About Preparation, the Process, and the Journey

It is all about preparation. It is a process. It is the journey of your lifetime. You will experience periods along the way when you're fulfilling your purpose and living your passion to a degree. But as I look back over sixty-eight years of my life and eagerly look ahead to the next twenty or so years ahead of me, I realize all that my life has prepared me for is converging into a higher place of purpose than I have experienced thus far. I believe that is by design. I believe that as we grow older and enter our "golden years," we have the opportunity to see a powerful convergence of our knowledge, our experiences, our wisdom, and our wilderness seasons that usher us into a greater place of influence and impact in this world. That is, if we will recognize it and embrace it.

The things I endured in my wilderness seasons have become a platform from which to speak my truth and help others find their truth. My wilderness seasons have taught me so much, and the pearls of wisdom I gleaned are so precious. They were rough roads to walk, but I wouldn't be who I am now without them. They prepared me for greater things.

When I was thirty-five years old, I attended a women's retreat. After the minister delivered the message, many of us went to the front to receive prayer. The speaker prayed for me.

She said, "This night is a new beginning for you. God has plans for you, and there is a future and a hope for you. Know that the desires you have are there because God has put them there, and He will bring them to pass. You have stood strong and stood well, so keep standing for there are plans for you that you have not even begun to see. But these things are not yet, for God is nurturing you. Keep standing strong."

This was many years ago, and yet I feel that I am just now stepping fully into those plans that God was speaking about that night. Notice the words, "keep standing." This is what we all need to remember when we feel like the desires and passions of our hearts are not being realized. We are being nurtured and prepared for greater things to come. We are always moving toward greater things as we stand strong and continue our journey. Even in the wilderness seasons, we are growing and becoming more of who we are. Let it happen. Live each moment as it comes and keep standing, keep growing, keep moving forward.

You can't leave out the preparation time. You can't skip the wilderness seasons. They are crucial to your growth into the fullest version of yourself. Walking out on the center stage of your life means that you have emerged from the wilderness complete, whole, and perfect as you! This only happens through preparation, change, struggle, and perseverance in the good and tough times. All your life has purpose. Nothing is wasted.

JEWELS ARE FORMED IN THE WILDERNESS

A couple of days before my fifty-seventh birthday, I was sitting quietly in meditation and prayer when I saw an amazing picture and heard this beautiful message:

Jesus and I are sitting on the ground in the woods by a stream. We face each other, sitting cross-legged. He digs something up from the ground. He has a jewel in his hand. He brushes off the dirt and holds it up to the light. It is incredibly beautiful and blue with many facets.

He said, "This is a jewel of very great value and worth. It is formed only under tremendous pressure and heat over time, hidden from view. It's the jewel of suffering, and when you say yes to me—to whatever My will is for you and you lay down your plans and say yes to Me, this jewel begins to form. It's in your heart—it is your heart. It's blue for the revelation of the mysteries and depths of My wisdom that is only revealed in suffering and the testing of fiery trials. When you take this jewel into your heart, it glows bright green. That stands for life—My life that I bring forth out of those deep times of suffering and pain, as you continue to abide in Me even during your trials. I am refining you, my daughter, and it is all for a purpose."

And then a little over a year later, this message came through:

"Pearls are formed through trials and tribulations, a piece of dirt, a foreign substance not meant for you, but it enters your life and gets embedded in your soul. I take that intruder and turn it into a precious treasure over time. It is hidden for a time and revealed only when the fullness of time is complete. Each pearl is unique in its qualities, and each is given to the world to show forth My glory and to add to the filling up of the body—to fully equip and adorn her. You are a part of this adorning, and it is time to bring this pearl out of hiding."

I have come out of hiding. I am coming out of the wilderness as a pearl, refined and ready to shine on that stage. I look back on these messages and these points in my life and see the refining process preparing me for this time in my life.

As you can see from these messages, I was encouraged to know that all that I was experiencing in the different seasons of my life were preparing me for greater things. I am sharing these messages with you because they illustrate how powerful and beautiful our wilderness seasons can be.

If you stop fighting them and let them be, you will have an entirely different experience. Can you see that you are being formed as a pearl or a stunning jewel as you walk through your wilderness? There is deeper work going on inside. There are incredible gifts to be discovered in the desert times of life.

Allow me to share the story of one of these wilderness seasons.

Years ago, my husband and I operated a nonprofit teen center, but when the funding dried up, we looked for an alternative way to provide a safe and fun place for the youth in our area to hang out. We decided to open that family fun center I told you about in Chapter 1. It was to be a skating rink with laser tag, arcade games, and bounce houses for the younger children. The idea was that if the business would provide the income, we would not need to rely on donations to keep it going. This would be a family fun center that would bless our entire community. It was an exciting idea, but we didn't have the money to fund such a project. We needed a partner.

My husband met a man who said he wanted to build this center for us and help us get it established. The deal was that we would work hard to buy out his shares in five years and own the business totally. This was our retirement plan. Build this business to be something wonderful—a fun, wholesome family fun center that our entire community could enjoy for years to come.

I remember vividly the day we signed the loan papers and our business agreement with our partners (there were now two) after much negotiation and thousands of dollars paid to our lawyer to ensure that our interests were protected in this agreement. The original agreement had been extremely stacked against us and in the favor of our partners, but our attorney had managed to fix some of the major problems in the deal. I had a sick feeling in my stomach that day. We were new to the business world, and it was obvious that our partners knew it and took advantage of that fact. The whole thing felt wrong. I told my husband how I felt, but he believed it would all work out for us. We were already so deep into this thing. He believed we could make it work.

We signed the papers and became two of four guarantors on this million-dollar SBA business loan. The center was built, and we opened our doors to an excited public in May 2005. It was thrilling to build something so beautiful and fun. We loved welcoming all the smiling faces as they came through the doors ready to have a good time with their family and friends. We hired a staff of high school and college kids and enjoyed pouring into them and helping them learn skills and gain work experience on their first job. One young man was only fifteen when we hired him. He had a physical handicap, but he didn't let that dampen his enthusiasm. He was all in and set about learning every aspect of our center. He was an outstanding worker and eventually was promoted to manager. Helping these young people develop character and a strong work ethic was one of the greatest rewards of running that business.

We consistently struggled with our financial partners. From day one, they pressured us and demanded a return on investment. Without going into all the sad details, I can tell you that the conflict with them came to a head one day when one of the partners marched in and demanded that we leave. He was taking over the operations. This move violated our operating agreement, but we decided it was in our best interest to settle with these partners and get out of the business rather than continue to fight with them. After a long battle and thousands of dollars in attorney fees, we finally came to a settlement. One part of that agreement required them to refinance the loan and remove our names as guarantors. That never happened.

For the next nine years, we lived with that loan hanging over our heads. The partner who took over eventually defaulted on the loan and closed the business. It was only a matter of time before the SBA would come looking for their money from all the guarantors. The day came when we received notice from the SBA that we owed them over a half million dollars. We prepared for bankruptcy, thinking that was the only way out of this mess. But a miracle happened.

We reached out to the SBA and offered a deal based on what they would receive in bankruptcy. They don't usually do deals. One person told me that they will take everything you have if they need to. They don't care about you. They just want their money.

God cares, though. We had been praying all those years for justice and for us to be released from this debt. The SBA came through with a deal, and it was less than we offered! We paid it and were finally free of this weight on our shoulders. That was an amazing feeling. It took some time for the reality to sink in. I had to keep reminding myself that we no longer needed to wait for that shoe to drop. It was gone.

But this had been a nine-year wilderness season. All that time, we had been carrying the weight of this debt, knowing that at any time, we would receive that letter. After the letter came, it was another two years before the whole thing was settled.

On many mornings I sat on the edge of my bed in a complete state of panic, feeling like I was on the edge of a cliff about to fall into the dark abyss below. I feared we would lose our home and savings and everything we had worked for, and we were no longer young. We didn't have the luxury of starting over. If I let my thoughts dwell there, I stayed in that state of panic. But I learned to shift my state of mind from the future (that wasn't real) to the present moment (that was real) and remind myself that right now, we were still in our home, and all was well. I didn't know how it would all work out, but I brought myself back to a place of trust, knowing that God had always been faithful to us, and He would be in this situation as well.

I share this story with you because it was a long and stressful ordeal for us, but there were many pearls formed through it.

Pearl 1: I developed the practice of being present in the moment—how to live in the *now* and not in an uncertain, unreal future.

Pearl 2: Endurance and resilience grew stronger in me. I did not sit paralyzed by fear of what might happen. I learned to keep moving toward my goals and act even when I did not feel like it.

Pearl 3: I learned to trust in the faithfulness of God and that He is always working things out for my good and for His purposes in my life.

The wilderness season can do that for you. There is no reason to fear or resist the struggles of your life. There are precious gifts there if you look for them. There are excellent and profound truths to uncover. Your perseverance, resilience, courage, and faith are refined into pure gold in the fires of your trials. It isn't easy, nor very pleasant or enjoyable, but the results are entirely worth it.

How you walk through your wilderness seasons and the person you become depends on you. How you experience these times and how you emerge from them are determined by how you view them. It is all about perspective. What lenses are you viewing your difficulties through? How are you framing them in your thoughts and the words you speak over your life? That makes all the difference in the world. You can emerge transformed, a stronger and wiser person, or you can crawl out barely alive. It is up to you.

There is an exercise in the STAR Guide called My Wilderness Wonders. Use it to discover the pearls and jewels that your wilderness experiences have created for you. You may be amazed at what you discover.

One of the most powerful ways to emerge transformed is to hear your heart's true story.

Access the Digital Workbook: https://bit.ly/StarGuideWorkbook
or the Paperback Workbook: https://amzn.to/3JUkchQ

CHAPTER 7

HEAR YOUR HEART'S TRUE STORY

*You either walk inside your story and own it or you stand
outside your story and hustle for your worthiness.*

~ Brené Brown

*I will greatly rejoice in the Lord, my soul shall be joyful
in my God; for he hath clothed me with the garments
of salvation, he hath covered me with the robe of righ-
teousness, as a bridegroom decketh himself with orna-
ments, and as a bride adorneth herself with her jewels.*

~Isaiah 61:10

FROM MY JOURNAL (AGE 30)

This was a word spoken over me by my pastor at the time. I was
still married to my first husband who was also the man who had
trafficked me. At the time this was spoken to me, it had only been

four years since I had escaped prostitution. I had not received any counseling or therapy. I had not told anyone about it. Only my husband knew.

"I'd say to you, my daughter, that you've known turmoil and you've known turning and twisting within you. And you've cried out and said God, I don't understand the changes and the twisting and the hurting. But I would say to you, daughter, to know that healing is coming forth on your behalf for My glory and for your blessing.

"And yes, daughter, even recently there has been healing coming forth because you have been a woman who has been torn and you said God, I feel as one who has been in two worlds. I feel like I'm a part of two worlds, and I don't understand it all. Receive that healing and deliverance by faith, and allow me to restore dignity as never before, allow me to restore confidence as never before, and allow me to restore worth in your life as never before. Because I desire to use you as never before. I desire not only to bless you and rain down blessings upon you and yours but also to bless others through you.

"So know that you've been one who has been torn between two worlds, but know that my power is sufficient to bring healing and restoration, and I will bring oneness and a wholeness to your spirit that you've never known before as a woman, and in that, you will be able to minister to others and you will be able to say, 'Truly I know the confusion that you've had because I've been there, but my God has healed and delivered me and made me sound and now, through His grace, I can minister effectively to others to receive that healing—receive ministry of my Spirit.'"

OUR INNER STORIES DEFINE US

When this word was spoken over me, I was married to the man who had trafficked me in Las Vegas. We were married a year after I was rescued out of the prostitution. Our daughter was born in 1983 and at the time I received this word, she was almost a year old. You may wonder why I married him after all he had put me through. I was still living in my trauma fog. I still believed I was unworthy of love. Who else would want me? I may as well marry him. If I don't, I'll never get married. That's how my thought process went.

I was living in two realities, in turmoil and a turning and twisting within me, just as this word said. It was a prophetic word, meaning that the pastor was saying what he heard from God about me. The pastor did not know my story. He didn't know me at all. But God did. And God knew my true story was to be a story of redemption. My new story would be one of restoration—the restoration of my worth, dignity, and confidence. That story is now my reality.

I still have that word as it was originally written on paper, by my husband at the time, if you can believe it. He had no idea what it meant. I felt the truth of it in my heart, but in my mind, I was confused. I couldn't see how I would ever be healed and delivered. I didn't know how I would ever know that I am valuable and precious or how I could ever be whole again. But I held fast to that word. It was my heart's true story.

I told myself other stories over the years before I went through my healing journey. I believed stories that I wasn't valuable or worthy. I believed that no one wanted to hear what I had to say. I believed I should stay quiet and in the background. I believed I had a shameful past and that if anyone knew about it, they would reject me.

What are the stories you tell yourself about who you are? We all have those stories. They usually start in childhood. We interpret what's happening around us and what is being said to us and about us. We accept those interpretations as being true about who we are, and they gradually become interwoven into the tapestry of our core identity.

We believe the stories and we become the stories. From there, they become self-fulfilling prophecies as our life is created by our beliefs and thoughts. Our actions and choices are then aligned with those beliefs, and we literally become who we think we are.

We don't realize what is happening. Many people live their entire lives inside those stories, never discovering their true selves or fulfilling their true potential. To me, this is the most tragic thing that can happen in life. Even more tragic than suffering heartache and loss, abuse and neglect, injury, disease, and pain. I believe the most tragic thing in life is not becoming who you truly are and never living out your purpose. Even in our times of suffering and loss, we can grow through those times of adversity. But if we are not being true to our core identity, our difficult seasons will define us as victims rather than conquerors.

It all starts with a story. Our stories to ourselves are like embedded data on the hard drive of our heart. They drive everything we think, feel, and do. The good news is that those stories can be rewritten. Your heart can be reprogrammed so that your inner stories are in sync with your true, amazing self. When that happens, you step into your power, and that life force flows from you with an ease and a freedom you never thought possible. You can't take your heart to a heart-reprogramming center to have the hard drive rewired. Only one person can do that—you! Only you can reprogram your heart and rewrite your inner stories.

Let the Old Stories Go, and Live in the Truth

Through my experiences and working with many clients through the years, I have identified five steps to this process of hearing your heart's true story. If you follow all five of these phases, you will manifest a new story in your life. Your new story will become your new reality.

One Inner Story Revealed

I remember vividly the day I uncovered one of my inner stories. I sat on the floor, my back against the wall, my Bible and journal open in front of me. Beautiful, peaceful music wafted through the air softly, inviting all of us in the room into the quiet and stillness. I looked around the room at the other women, doing the same as I was. Some were lying down, some were on their knees, some sitting, some standing, all deep in communion with the Lord. A holy hush filled the place as we were wrapped in God's loving presence.

Inside, I was anything but peaceful and serene. There was a tug-of-war going on underneath the surface, an inner turmoil of confusion and fear. It was a battle between one of my old inner stories and a new fiery passion beckoning me to step out into my calling. I had been feeling a consistent pull that I was being called to speak to women's groups, to lead from the front of the room, at retreats and meetings like the one I was attending that weekend. This feeling had been growing in intensity and was becoming more insistent, and there was an excitement behind it. But the old inner story kept throwing a heavy wet blanket over that excitement, threatening to extinguish those flames of passion, turning them to ashes.

The story had me rooted to a deep belief that I was not good enough or interesting enough to hold anyone's attention as a speaker or teacher. The story line went like this: "Who would want to listen to you? What do you have to say that anyone would want to listen to? You would bore them to tears! You're a nobody. No one cares about you! You need to stay in the background because no one notices you or sees you or is interested in your thoughts or ideas." The suffocating pressure of those words pressed my heart against the wall as I sat there, paralyzed by fear. Our stories are made up of words, and words are powerful, especially the ones we speak to ourselves.

The desire was still there and tugged at my heart to be brave, to dare to believe, to take a chance and speak up. My Bible was open to 2 Timothy 1:7, which says, *"For God hath not given us the spirit of fear; but of power, and of love, and of a sound mind."* As I wrestled with the fear created by the old story to stay in the background and be quiet against the intense pull of this exciting desire to be who I'm called to be, I heard a voice shout to me loud and clear—almost audibly, it was so real: "Stop it! Stop being timid. Stop shrinking back in fear! It's time for you to step out of the shadows."

I was shaken to my core. This was a pivotal fork-in-the-road, line-in-the-sand kind of moment. My heart stood at attention as I became keenly alert to the fact that I had a choice. I could continue to embrace the old story and stay attached to the wall or I could ditch the timidity and receive the spirit of love, power, and sound mind that had been given to me. When someone gives you a gift, you need to reach out and take it to make it yours. It was like God was standing there in front of me, handing me this gift and invitation to come up to a better, higher place, to answer the call on my life, to fulfill the purpose He has for me. He had to shout it into my soul to pierce the dense fog of that old message I had believed for so long.

As I stood on the precipice of that moment, I made my choice. As my heartbeat wildly inside my chest and my stomach flipped,

I said yes. My next thought was, "What do I do first?" I knew my first step. I was to share a scripture and a message that God was ready to give me for the women at this retreat. I was to write it down and give it to one of the leaders to share with the group, if they felt it was appropriate. The leaders had been asking us to share anything we heard as we were seeking God if we felt it was for the group. So, I wrote out the verses and the message I heard, and with a quivering heart, I handed it to one of the leaders.

I was so nervous and anxious that I thought I might throw up. What if they rejected it? What if they decided it wasn't a message from God for the group? How would that feel? I was afraid that it would just confirm that old story that I should just keep quiet; no one wanted to hear anything I had to say. That would mean that I was not hearing from God, and that call to become a speaker and leader was just a fairy tale, something I had made up. I didn't know if my heart could take that rejection. I had felt overlooked and rejected for so many years. I had felt like I didn't really belong most of my life, and now look what I had done. What was I thinking? How could I have put myself out there like that? I know it sounds silly that I went through so much consternation over that one note, but the battle was real. A war raged inside my heart. It seemed like a matter of life or death to me in that moment.

The group reconvened as we moved into the next part of the retreat. Women filed back into the room and settled into their seats. Announcements were made. The music began and we stood to worship. Then the leader came to the front of the room to start the meeting.

The battle continued to rage within me. My pulsed raced, my heart pounded in my ears, and I felt a little nauseated. I took a few deep breaths. I settled back into prayer. The storm began to calm, and my whirling thoughts began to quiet. My pulse slowed, my jaw loosened, my body relaxed. Then my heart said to me,

"Whatever the outcome, you did it! You took the step. You faced the fear and bravely obeyed God, and He is pleased with you. That's all that matters." Relief washed over me. I felt at peace, and whether that message was ever shared or not, all was well. I had broken through a barrier, a smoke screen of fear. This was a huge victory.

The leader told us that there were a few words that some of the women had given to them. She said that they had prayed over them and felt that a couple were for the group, and some were for individuals or for a different time. My heart skipped a beat. Which category did mine fall into? Hush! Be still! It didn't matter. All was well no matter what. Deep breath.

She said that there was one particular message that they felt was a powerful word for the group and for this exact time. Then she began to read. My heart leaped. I couldn't believe my ears. She was reading *my* message. Oh! My goodness!

Joy filled my soul, and I felt the bonds of that old story snap apart and fall away from my heart. I do hear from God! I do have something to say that would inspire and encourage others. I had stepped over that line in the sand to answer a call on my life, and God was confirming it in a big way, almost like those airplanes at the beach that fly over and write a message in the sky for all to see. The message read: "Yes, Janelle, you are called to speak up. You have a message to share, and it has value. People need to hear it!"

My Heart's True Story Emerged

That was the beginning of a new season for me. It marked my soul deeply. I discovered how powerful those old stories can be and how deeply embedded they are in our souls. It was only a first step, but I had broken through a massive barrier by choosing to believe that the old story simply wasn't true. It was a false identity I had accepted years earlier, and it had defined my life. A new realization dawned on me that I have power over what I believe. I can believe the old story and stay stuck, or I can receive the truth of who I am as God spoke it into my heart and rewrite the story. It changed my life.

I didn't immediately begin a speaking career and no, invitations to speak at retreats and conferences did not start pouring in. Those old stories often have tentacles that reach deep into your soul. You must dig to the roots and pull them all out. Some stories won't go deep, but the deep ones impact your life the most, so it is best to uproot those first.

A word of caution here: if your deep stories are rooted in trauma or abuse, please do not do this work alone. Work with a professional who knows how to walk with you through the process and guide you safely to a healthy place.

INNER STORIES BEGIN AS SEEDS

One thing I've noticed about inner stories is that often, if they are not linked to traumatic events, they start quite innocently. It isn't that something tragic or bad happened, it is how you viewed it and the meaning you placed on it that created the root for the story.

As children, we didn't have the capacity to understand or express what we felt. We couldn't understand the conclusions we established in our hearts about what was happening around us or to us. So, the seed of these beliefs was planted in our hearts and began to grow, and no one knew. We didn't even know.

Our hearts are a mystery. They hold many secrets, but that doesn't mean they can't be uncovered and understood.

This is a journey of discovery, and the treasure you find is well worth the effort. My observation is that most people either don't realize this or don't want to take that journey. It seems daunting, intimidating, and overwhelming. I know this is true because that is exactly how I felt. That is why it took over thirty-five years for me to embark on that journey.

How do you embark on this journey of knowing yourself and uncovering your inner stories?

Step One:
Unearth the Stories You're Telling Yourself

That day at the retreat, I discovered a story. It was revealed to me through prayer and reading scripture. It came into my consciousness because I was seeking it. I wanted to know why I felt such turmoil.

It starts with a desire to be whole. Then you seek it out. Go inward. Your answers are there, inside your heart. Listen to your heart. Meditation and prayer are the best disciplines to hear what your heart is trying to tell you.

For me, it is usually a small nudge. A thought keeps softly tapping on my mind. It is exceptionally soft—polite, really. I can ignore it if I want, but it will come back. A thought pops up in my mind at random times. I've learned to tune in to those thoughts. When I was seeking the root of this story, the story that said no one wanted to hear anything I had to say, a memory from my early childhood kept showing up on the screen of my mind. At first, I dismissed it, thinking that it was such a non-event that it couldn't possibly have anything to do with this story. It insisted, so I finally paid attention.

You can ask yourself this question: what's the story I'm telling myself that is now too small for who I am becoming?

The story I told you in Chapter 4 when I was having dinner at my friend's house and my dad was calling for me was one of these "inner story seeds." When my dad stopped calling for me, the thought seed planted in my heart was "I am not important enough for Dad to keep looking for me." A feeling of abandonment accompanied that thought. There's no memory of me saying anything, just the feeling and the thought.

As a child, I didn't have the maturity to understand or express what I was feeling. It just landed there and took root. However, that thought was a lie. The truth was that my mom told my dad where I was, so that's why he stopped calling for me. The thought and the feeling were not true, but I believed the story on a very subconscious level, and this thread began to weave into the fabric of my core identity. I was not important and easily forgotten and overlooked.

It was difficult at first for me to believe that this memory was the root of this story, but I finally decided to trust my heart. This was the memory that my heart brought to me persistently. As I listened to my heart for more, two other childhood memories came up.

One occurred when I was in the first grade. I had walked into my classroom after visiting the bathroom. My skirt was tucked into my panties, and I didn't realize it. My classmate who had gone to the bathroom with me had seen it, though, and was giggling as I walked into the room. The classroom erupted in laughter. My teacher called me over to her and gently fixed my skirt. I wanted to disappear.

The thread of the story grew thicker and longer. I was not important enough for my classmate to protect me from that humiliation. Instead, I was someone to be laughed at—I was a joke. Unfortunately, some kids can be cruel, so many of our inner stories start because of childhood meanness and bullying.

The second memory was from the second grade. I was in a daydream in the middle of a lesson. I tended to let my mind drift in class. I suddenly became aware that my teacher was calling my name. I attended a Catholic school, and my teacher seemed like a towering, intimidating figure dressed from head to toe in a long black habit, the term for a nun's attire. She told me to come to her. She then proceeded to tweak my ear in front of the class and said something about not listening. Again, I wanted to disappear. The story became more entrenched in my heart. I was someone to laugh at—I was a joke. I was not important.

Fast forward to my early teens to another key memory. I'm sitting at the table eating dinner with my large family. There were eight of us kids and my parents all talking at once. I was trying to say something, but no one heard me. No one paid attention to me at all. In my frustration, I turned to the wall and started talking out loud. This caused everyone to stop and look at me. Someone asked me what I was doing. I patiently explained that I was talking to the wall because no one would listen to me. At least the wall listened to me. They laughed and then went back to chattering away. No one asked me what it was that I was trying to say. So, the story continued to grow in my heart that I was not important, not interesting, and not worth anyone's attention or care.

My chat with the wall became a family joke because it is comical. I can laugh along with them about it because I know that there was no ill intent on their part. They didn't think I was not important. They weren't purposely ignoring me out of disinterest or not caring about me. We were a big, noisy family.

Honestly, when I look at each of those memories, I realize that by themselves, they are not anything major. No tragedy or trauma took place. They were typical events that happen in a typical life. Children are not nice to each other; frustrated and tired teachers get impatient with students who are daydreaming—although they never should embarrass or humiliate children like that—and family dinners can be noisy and chaotic—at least in big families like mine!

The reality is, though, that our inner stories usually begin that way. They start from seemingly uneventful and normal situations. Our interpretations of those situations create our false stories, but we can unravel them and rewrite the stories with truth as our foundation. These are the stories that make up our core identities. When those stories are based on lies, our true identity becomes obscured, and we are left in the awkward and vulnerable position of trying to be someone we are not because we don't really know who we are.

We start wearing a mask and building walls. Our stories seem so real, and we see more "evidence" that makes us believe they are true. They become self-fulfilling prophecies. As more events happen in life, we continue to interpret them considering the inner story that has been growing through the years.

Every time someone interrupted me in a conversation or didn't hear me when I spoke, it added to my belief in the story. I grew timid about speaking up, voicing my opinions, or sharing my thoughts. I developed the tendency to mumble and talk so quietly that no one could hear me. And of course, that just reinforced this belief that I had nothing worthwhile to say. Do you see the vicious cycle?

What is the core story that holds you back the most?

Most of us have that one story that shows up consistently. It is usually tied to your strongest passion and to your life purpose, that very thing you are created and designed to do. The most powerful inner stories are the ones that tell us we are not good enough to do that very thing we most want to do.

That is the story you need to start unraveling first. This is the one you need to rewrite first. You won't ever be able to be the star of your own story unless you deal with that one core story. You know what it is. Your heart knows it very well!

As Brené Brown said, "Not only do we need to own our story and love ourselves in the process, we have to figure out the real story!"[20]

Step Two:
Listen to Your Heart

Once you have uncovered your inner stories and dug down to their roots, the next step is to listen deeply to discover your heart's true story. Your new story must be grounded in the truth of your core identity. You just need to hear your heart when it speaks to you.

I have experienced many amazing messages from my heart, but I didn't realize what they were for a long time. I dismissed them as random and seemingly irrelevant thoughts that popped into my mind at the oddest times. I eventually learned to listen and consider these thoughts as my heart possibly talking to me. As I learned to tune in to that frequency, like you would tune in to a radio station, I discovered a whole universe of wisdom and guidance. I believe my heart speaks to me as God's Spirit directs it. If I'll pay attention, those nuggets of wisdom and truth will float to the surface of my consciousness, waiting for me to pluck like ripe fruit.

For years, my heart told me that I was meant for more. When I began to listen to my heart, I took a deep breath, listened, and asked questions. Slowly, I began to realize that the reason this idea seemed so ridiculous to me was that I had that inner story still running in the background. The story that what I had to say was not interesting or valuable to anyone else. The story that told me no one wanted to listen to anything I had to say.

The old story had to go so the new story could emerge. And just as the old story was constructed slowly over time, changing your inner stories takes time. You need to sow some seeds again and nurture them so they can take root, grow, and blossom into your new reality. You must receive those new seeds and embrace them.

Often, for the old stories to be released and new stories to emerge, you must let go of shame. Shame keeps our old stories locked up because we are afraid to face them, speak them out loud, and own them. That's how the old stories keep us trapped in those places of timidity and holding back.

Brené Brown's books and her research were instrumental for me in this process of owning my story, speaking about it out loud, looking at it face to face, and then realizing that those stories didn't have to define me or continue to impact my present or my future. I finally came to the place where I could fully own my story—to unlock the prison where it had festered and haunted me. I chose to bring it out into the open where God could blow His healing wind upon it. I found I was able to let go of the shame that surrounded it.

Brené Brown said, "Shame needs three things to grow out of control in our lives: secrecy, silence, and judgment. When something shaming happens and we keep it locked up, it festers and grows. It consumes us. We need to share our experience. Shame happens between people, and it heals between people. If we can find someone who has earned the right to hear our story, we need to tell it. Shame loses power when it is spoken. In this way, we need to cultivate our story to let go of shame, and we need to develop shame resilience in order to cultivate our story."[21]

Before I could write my new story on my heart, I had to break off the shame and stop hiding my past. Brené Brown said shame loses its power when it is spoken. I discovered that she is correct.

I had to share my past experiences out loud with someone if I wanted to let go of the shame and cultivate my new true story. I began sharing my past with trusted confidants who I knew would hold space for me without judgment. Gradually, my confidence grew, and the grip of shame lessened. The final blow to that shame happened when I shared my prostitution story publicly for the first time at our women's retreat. Remember the story I told about taking that brave step and sharing a word with our leaders in a retreat? That was when my new story began to emerge, which was that I was meant to speak and lead from the front. My heart told me that I would be teaching from the front of the room at our women's retreats one day.

That day came and here I was, teaching from the front of the room at our retreat about a couple of years later, in the very same room. This time, I publicly shared the greatest shame story of my life. The chains fell away for good that day. It was not easy. I was shaking all over, from head to foot. My heart pounded in my chest, and my stomach flipped. I thought I would faint at one point. But I was surrounded by women who loved me and supported me. They held me with their strong, compassionate hearts as I finally released that festering, shame-ridden story from the dark corners of my heart where it had been embedded for decades.

After my talk, back at my seat, I stood as we all sang a worship song, my hands raised high in victory. I experienced a physical sensation of being ten feet tall. I felt like a towering giant, a warrior who had slain her worst enemy. It was an incredible experience but following on the heels of that sensation came a rush of shame thoughts. "Why did you share that? Are you crazy? They are all going to think you are a disgrace! No one will want to be your friend now. You have totally blown it. Now it's all out in the open, and you'll never be able to stand tall again." Those messages came like a barrage of fiery darts aimed straight for my heart.

I fought them off as best I could for the next few minutes until we were released to lunch. I didn't know what to expect. Would

I be shunned and ignored? Would the women look at me with disdain in their eyes?

It didn't take long for me to find out. As we filed out of the room and headed for the cafeteria, one woman walked with me and thanked me for having the courage to share my story. She said it helped her to know that she, too, could open up and be vulnerable. As the afternoon progressed, more women came to tell me the same thing. After our small group sessions, stories emerged, and women let go of their own shame stories and received prayer, encouragement, and freedom. They all said they could do so because I had shared mine, and it gave them the courage and the permission to do the same.

Shame is released when experiences are shared with trusted people. However, even though I shared my story publicly, that doesn't mean you have to stand in front of a room and tell yours. It's vital, though, that you find a trustworthy person who will hold your story in a safe, nonjudgmental environment so your heart can find healing.

Now the stage was set for me to move on to the next step in writing my new, truthful core story. I could now fully embrace who I am.

STEP THREE: EMBRACE YOUR HEART'S TRUE STORY

"If we want to live fully, without the constant fear of not being enough, we have to own our story," Brené Brown said.[22]

Your heart will reveal to you your new story, the one that is meant for you. It may take you by surprise at first because you've believed the old one for so long—probably your whole life. It's hard to change that narrative because it has become embedded.

It's sort of like hearing a fairy tale like *Little Red Riding Hood* with a new ending where the wolf isn't even in the story. If you heard it, you'd immediately dismiss it as the wrong story. You might even argue with the person telling the story and list reasons why that new story is not real. The story you've heard your whole life is real to you. But when you stop to think about it, you realize that the original *Little Red Riding Hood* was created in the mind of the author. It isn't a true story—it's just made up, and it can be changed.

The same is true for your inner stories. You created them in your mind based on your interpretation of the event that caused them in the first place. They became your truth as you heard them repeatedly in your mind. It isn't easy to accept that it isn't a true story at all. It's just your version of a fairy tale.

You first need to be open to that possibility. Consider that the stories you've been telling yourself about who you are were not based on truth. Your deeper heart knows the truth about who you are. As this new, true story begins to emerge, it may seem preposterous at first. But as you examine those old inner stories, question whether they are true, and look at how they are holding you back, you'll begin to see that it's time to let them go.

When you let go of the old stories, your heart will gently and persistently bring your true story to the surface. What was once invisible can now show itself. Who you truly are and what you're meant to do in this world will finally emerge. You begin to see it and feel it. It's the real you. It's what you're truly called to. It's aligned with your strengths, gifts, passions, and personality. This true story shows up on the screen of your mind. Your heart is projecting it there almost like a movie. Your heart speaks to you, "*This* is the real you!"

Now it's time to embrace it. Open your heart to the possibility that even though it may *seem* impossible and unfathomable, be open. Even though you can't see *how* that could ever come to be, be open anyway. My heart consistently showed me a vision of me speaking on a stage to hundreds of women. I dismissed it repeatedly because it seemed impossible. I couldn't figure out *how* that would ever happen. I am in my sixties and just now starting to write and speak. There isn't enough time for me to be so well-known that hundreds of women would come to hear me speak. And why would they? Who am I to speak on stages to huge audiences?

That's where my thoughts went in the beginning, when my heart began to project that vision onto the screen of my mind. My heart was persistent, though, and the vision continued to show up at the most random times.

Finally, it dawned on me that I don't need to know the "how" right now. I realized that it won't happen if I don't first embrace it as a possibility and let it become my new story. I opened my heart to the possibility instead of rejecting it. Once I began to do that, I found myself believing that it could happen one day. If I am meant to speak on a large stage and impact hundreds of women with my message, then it will happen, but I must believe it first.

You must believe in your new story first. If you don't believe in it, no one else will. I chose to embrace this vision as my new story. The old story that no one wants to hear anything I have to say has been discarded, and this new story has taken root. I have no idea when that vision will become a reality, but that is not important right now. What matters right now is that I have embraced this as my new and very real story.

The next thing I realized is that there is more to this process than just being open and embracing the new story. That is only the beginning. The seeds have been planted. Now they must be watered and nurtured so they can grow and become visible for all to see. This meant that it was time for me to declare my new story to the world.

Step Four:
Shout It from the Rooftops

Have you ever noticed that once you speak something out or write it down, it seems much more real than when it was just a thought in your mind? That's because words are powerful. Studies in the field of neuroscience have learned that words impact our brains, our emotions, and our bodies.

This is the reason affirmations are so powerful. When you write down the words that describe who you are and what you want to do in your life, then say them out loud, you are creating new pathways in your brain—you are establishing new real estate in your heart and mind.

I began to tell people my new story. I wrote it down. I visualized myself speaking on stages. I began growing new pathways in my brain. My new story was taking shape, and it was changing my life.

Step Five:
Do the Work

If you don't tend your garden, the plants will die. You can talk all you want about what you've planted in your garden—the tomatoes, corn, beans, potatoes, and all the wonderful potential food that has been sown in the soil. However, any farmer or gardener will tell you that if that is all you do, you will never see those vegetables come to the surface, grow, and produce fruit. You must do the work in your garden to bring forth all that delicious food.

This is where the rubber meets the road. This is where so many dreams die. If you never act on your dreams, they will remain just that—dreams. Dreams are images that help us visualize what we want, and they are important. The more clearly that we can visualize what we want to create, the better. We must have something to aim at, a target we want to hit, a finish line we want to cross, and dreams give us that. If you don't plan your garden and know exactly what vegetables you want to grow or how you want your flowers to look, then you won't know what seeds to plant where.

I am not a gardener, I must confess. Once I planted a bunch of flower seeds randomly in my yard with no plan and no idea of what it would look like once the flowers all grew and bloomed. The result was colorful but very chaotic and not very appealing. I had tall plants growing in front of short plants and flowers in the sun that should have been in the shade and no color scheme at all. I admire well-designed flower gardens. They are so beautiful and pleasing to the eye. I learned a valuable lesson that year, not only about planting a flower garden but manifesting anything I want in my life. If I want something to grow and bloom in my life, I need to have a vision for it and a plan.

Then I need to do the work. I need to act. The seeds won't plant themselves. They won't water themselves, feed themselves, or weed themselves. Once you embrace the new story your heart speaks to you, you must plant the seeds and do the work to bring those stories to life.

After I embraced the vision of speaking on stage, I started planting seeds. I thought about what I needed to do to position myself to be that speaker on a big stage. I took courses on public speaking. I joined a speaking club for women and then started one in my town. I wrote speeches and practiced them and received feedback. I rewrote them, presented them again, and received more feedback. I began learning how to find opportunities to speak, then I began asking if I could speak wherever there were platforms to do so, whether in person, on podcasts, or in online summits. I took lots of action and planted lots of seeds.

Those seeds took time to sprout. It was discouraging sometimes. There were days where it looked like I was wasting my time and energy. There were moments when I wondered what in the world I was doing. But my coach reminded me that I was planting seeds and watering them. They would sprout and grow if I continued doing the work.

Sure enough the seeds began to sprout. I now receive invitations to speak, and I know that more invitations will come. The opportunities are appearing more frequently, and the audiences are getting bigger. All that is exciting, of course, because I am manifesting that dream. But more wonderful than the size of the groups I am speaking to is the joy I'm experiencing each time I speak. I am fulfilled and energized by the connections with each group and by the knowledge that I am contributing something of value to their lives and the world.

My new story is being written with each new opportunity to speak. This story that my heart has given me is my true story taking root. The old story is fading away. I rarely ever hear that old tape in my head. The new story says that when I take center stage as the star of my own story, I am bringing a gift to the world. That gift is just being me. And not just being me, but being unapologetically me and loving who I am. The world needs me to be who I am. When I do that, and when you do that, we release a gift to the world that no one else can give.

You must tell your new story. Your story needs to be shouted from the rooftops! It must be written down and shared with the world. Your story is priceless and of extreme value to all of us. It must be written by you as you create a clear vision of what it looks like and then sow the seeds to bring it into reality.

Take some time now to work on the *Your Heart's True Story Blueprint* in the **STAR Guide** to create your new story framework.

Access the Digital Workbook: https://bit.ly/StarGuideWorkbook or the Paperback Workbook: https://amzn.to/3JUkchQ

PHASE THREE:

ACCEPT AND ACTIVATE

Scan the QR Code above with your Smartphone for
my message called Accept and Activate. Or, follow this link:
https://youtu.be/EvzD047mqNg

CHAPTER 8

DO YOU KNOW HOW GREAT YOU ARE?

We often have a diluted sense of self; we do not see the magnitude of the greatness inside of us. As a result, most people live within the parameters of the lowest part of their life; they dwell in the basement of their capability.[23]

~ Steve Maraboli

For we are his workmanship, created in Christ Jesus unto good works, which God hath before ordained that we should walk in them.

~ Ephesians 2:10

FROM MY JOURNAL (AGE 59)

Do you know how great you are? I'm calling you to be great and do great things because you are great in Me. Be who you are! Be renewed in the spirit of your mind, hearing the Spirit's words coming

from Me to you, thinking My thoughts, seeing from a heavenly per-
spective—from your seat in heavenly places. You are great—so be
great!

Do you see the greatness I've put inside you? Do you know your
name? It's important to know the name I've given you because it de-
scribes what I have woven into your DNA—your nature and your
character. I want you to know that I have a place and want to see
the good things in you that I have "knit into your innermost parts." I
have a divine record of your life in eternity. Do you know what it is?
I want to reveal your life in eternity so you can live today in the light
of who you are meant to become. I want you to see yourself from my
perspective and to hear what I say about you.

ACCEPT AND ACTIVATE

We have arrived at the third phase in the STAR Process:
Accept & Activate.

You've worked through a lot so far, and if you've done the work, you are ready now to unveil your beautiful, magnificent, uniquely designed true self. When you see her emerging from behind the curtain and walking out into the open, you will have no trouble accepting her with love and joy. Accepting yourself and loving who looks back at you in the mirror will put a spring in your step and energize you. Confidence will naturally grow because you'll believe in yourself, and you'll see limitless possibilities for your future. This phase is all about movement, stepping forward, action, and manifestation. Acceptance and activation—you are now well on your way down that path of destiny.

But first, you must answer this question: do you know how great you are?

This question rose from inside my spirit one day as I prepared to teach a women's Bible study. It came so clearly and suddenly that it surprised me and caused me to stop what I was doing and listen, as if someone were standing next to me tapping me on the shoulder.

I was perplexed. All I could answer was, "Me? I'm not all that great. I'm just an everyday kind of girl here, living an ordinary life." Over the next few days and even weeks, that question continued to show up. Finally, I asked God, "What do you mean?" A startling realization began to unfold in my heart, much like the turning pages of a book. As the sun rose above the horizon at the dawn of a new day, a marvelous and wonderful truth emerged in my soul, on the far edges of my comprehension.

I Am Fearfully and Wonderfully Made

There is a passage in the Bible, Psalm 139, that paints a vivid and magnificent description of how we have been fashioned by our Creator as beings made in His image and likeness. When you first read it, or even after reading it a hundred times, you scarcely can take it in. At least that has been my experience. I have read this psalm countless times in my forty years as a believer and mostly, I had let it leave surface brush strokes across my soul. It contains such beautiful imagery and evokes a sense of awe, that I could not fully comprehend it. This was *"knowledge too wonderful for me"* as the psalmist said in verse 6.

But what if it is true? What would happen if I knew this truth and embraced it fully? How would that change how I live and operate in this world? What if I lived as if it were true? That I am fearfully and wonderfully made—that there is greatness on the inside of me?

I began to consider that perhaps this psalm describes an unalterable and undeniable truth. If God created me in His image, then the result would be amazing, wouldn't it? Look at this verse:

"I will praise thee; for I am fearfully and wonderfully made: marvelous are thy works; and that my soul knoweth right well" (Psalm 139:14).

The word *fearfully* here means to fear, to revere, to be in awe.[3] *"Wonderfully made"* means to be distinct, marked out, set apart, and to show marvelous.[4] The phrase *"wonderful are thy works"* means that what God has made is surpassing, extraordinary, and marvelous.[5] What are those works? It's us! It's me! The word for *works* is the same word used in verse 15, the very next verse, when the psalmist said that he was "made" in secret and skillfully wrought in the womb. We are God's handiwork, His creation, and what He has made is extraordinary and marvelous. We are extraordinary and marvelous.

Do you know how great you are? Do you know that you are extraordinary, marvelous, awe-inspiring, and wonderful?

Every human being who has ever walked this earth has greatness on the inside of them. We are each created in the image and likeness of our Creator, so greatness is woven into the fabric of our being. I realized that I was interpreting the word *greatness* to mean something else. I was comparing myself to people who were great according to this world's definition of greatness. People who are rich or famous like Oprah Winfrey or have won Pulitzer Prizes or have sacrificed their lives to help

---

[3] (Strong n.d., 52)

[4] (Strong n.d., 94)

[5]

those who suffer, like Mother Theresa or Martin Luther King Jr. Those people are great, to be sure, but I came to understand what God was saying to me. He wanted me to know that this greatness is not reserved for only a few. We all have greatness inside of us because we are all His creation, and His works are wonderful. Those people allowed that greatness in them to be expressed and released through their life's work and so the world calls them great. What if we *all* did that?

God's definition of greatness is not the same as the world's definition. We have greatness on the inside of us, innately present in the form of potential. It's like a seed. Inside the seed is the potential for that plant to become what it was designed to become, whether that is a giant oak tree or a delicate rose bush. The potential is there, but it must be nurtured and watered and placed in the proper environment for it to grow and become all that it was meant to become.

It doesn't happen overnight. It takes preparation, planning, work, energy, and effort. There will be obstacles and battles. Many things can come against that oak tree or rose bush realizing their full potential. There may be droughts or floods. There may be insects that try to eat them or weeds that try to choke them out. There could be diseases that attack them as they try to grow. If they are tended to by a dedicated gardener, and if they persist through all that comes against them, they will one day realize their fullest potential.

We Have Seeds of Greatness Inside of Us

Those seeds hold the design and blueprint for who we are and what we are called to become and do in this world. When we nurture and grow those seeds to fully mature, we will manifest the greatness inside of us. When we fully embody our true selves and walk out the destiny placed on our lives, we will see that greatness manifested.

The greatness inside you does not make you better than other people. This isn't greatness that brings pride and arrogance. There is no comparison or competition in this greatness. It is more like being clothed in your rightful identity and being at home in your skin—being the star of *your* story, not someone else's.

When we walk in our own greatness, we make the world a better place. We shine our unique light that gives warmth to everyone around us and allows them to shine in their light as well. When we grow into the fullness of who we are, we contribute to this world. We take our rightful place and fill the gap that only we can fill. We complete the picture. I believe this is what the Bible means by the glory of the knowledge of God filling the whole earth. If every person walked in their own greatness, the earth would be full of the glory of God.

Knowing who you are is your quest, and it is vital that you stay on that journey. It is up to you to do it. No one can choose it for you. Getting to know yourself, loving who you are, and walking in your greatness is the most powerful and important thing you can do in your life. Sadly, though, many people never complete this quest, and many never take the first step.

For many women, this seems to be a mystery that eludes them. Why is it so difficult to connect who we are with what we do in this life? It seems like it should be easy, but it's not. Well-meaning, yet misguided, people tell us we shouldn't take a risk to go after our passions and dreams because it's not practical or "you can't make money doing that." We feel pressure to stay on the "safe track" in life and do what others think we should do. On top of that, the culture we've grown up in has told us that as women, we should tone things down. Don't be too assertive or you'll be viewed as bossy (or worse). Don't speak your mind or be too direct. Stay in the background, play small, and know your place "as a woman."

This is a great travesty. Women are full of amazing potential to have a massive impact in this world. Stop waiting for permission to be who you are. You must rise, shake off the dust of those limiting beliefs, discover your greatness, and be who you are. No one can take that from you. As Martin Luther King Jr. said, "Don't let anyone tell you that you are a nobody."

The primary obstacle that gets in the way of women walking in their true destiny and purpose is this: They are not dialed in to who they are first. It is like they are trying to walk out on the stage of their lives wearing the costumes of other actors instead of being in the role that fits them and them alone. They are not allowing their actions, aspirations, and goals to flow from a place of authenticity. They are acting rather than being. It takes a tremendous amount of energy and effort to do that.

When what you do flows from you being who you are, there's no force, and it feels like it is effortless. It doesn't feel like work. It feels like life and joy. It's like flowing with the current of a river. You don't have to fight, but when you're trying to do something that doesn't come from the core of who you are, it feels like work. It feels like you're swimming against the current.

For example, you take a job or jump into a business because it looks good, and maybe it has a lot of pieces to it that you like, but it's not aligned with your intricately God-woven design. You get bored and restless and you're unfulfilled. Or you struggle mightily because it is too challenging for you. It ends up feeling like effort.

I have been down that road many times. When we opened our family fun center, I had come straight out of teaching school for twenty years into running a business—with no prior experience, I might add! Crazy, huh? It was mostly my husband's dream, but I locked arms with him and wholeheartedly embraced this as our "dream business." I was one month shy of fifty-three when we opened our doors.

I was super excited about it. We knew nothing about the roller-skating business, but we immersed ourselves in learning everything about it, and we were committed to making this facility a success and a place for families to have fun together.

I thought it was going to be so fun to run this business and to see families and kids enjoying themselves in a place that we had designed for them. My passion for connection was in alignment with this business, and I thought I was called to do it at that point in my life. I felt a sense of elation knowing that we had created this place to serve our community, and people lined up at the door to experience what we had built for them.

A few months in, however, I began to struggle. The hours were long, and I was already exhausted. Rather than connecting with people, I was spending most of my time in the office doing all the necessary administrative tasks behind the computer. I was the office manager/HR director and the bookkeeper, too. While Bob was out on the rink enjoying being the DJ and talking with all our customers, watching them have fun, I was in the office crunching numbers, writing an employee manual, developing our policies, counting money, and scheduling parties. And though I was good at those tasks, none of them flowed out of my natural talents and strengths. My excitement quickly drained away along with my energy. I was also in the throes of menopause and experiencing all those symptoms. I was on edge, irritable, sleep-deprived, and suffering from constant hot flashes. It's no wonder I was barking at employees and customers and wondering who this person was inhabiting my body.

I began to experience panic attacks. Sometimes I couldn't breathe. It was like being on a merry-go-round that turned at a dizzying speed, and I had no way to get off the ride. I felt trapped and desperate. I wondered how I was going to keep this up for the next month, much less years until we retired.

Eventually, I settled into the routine and began to master all the skills needed to do my part. One of my favorite duties was developing the staff. I enjoyed building relationships with the high school and college kids we hired and teaching them job skills that would serve them for their whole lives. Things like integrity, respect, customer service, and working hard. I loved teaching them how to operate the cash register and settle their drawer at the end of a shift. Another part of my job that I enjoyed was setting up and running the birthday parties and teaching kids how to skate. But I was not happy. It felt like I constantly carried a heavy burden on my shoulders. Even at home or on vacation, we were still monitoring things at the skate center and getting calls from our staff.

When we ran into the huge conflict with our partners and decided to leave the business, I was saddened and angry about how it happened, but deep inside I felt tremendous relief. Although I loved our customers and employees, I was glad to be out from under the heavy load of running that business. It wasn't my dream, and it wasn't my passion. It had become a job, and it had taken over my life.

In contrast, I am now in year six of running my coaching and speaking business. Not once in the past six years have I experienced a panic attack or felt that this business was a heavy burden. Not one time have I wanted to quit or escape. Have I worked long hours? Yes, absolutely! Have there been difficulties and obstacles to overcome? You bet. Have there been times when I felt overwhelmed by all that I needed to do? Yes, of course. But not once have I felt like I didn't want to continue. It doesn't even feel like work most of the time. Even when I am working hard, it feels like I'm in the flow, doing what

I am meant to do, and it feels like satisfaction and fulfillment and passion.

That, my friends, makes all the difference in the world. Three years after we left that business, I was working as an office manager in an elementary school. I enjoyed my job, my boss, the people I worked with, and being around kids, but about a year into the job, I began to feel that restlessness again—not an all-out panic attack, but a restlessness. By this time, I was fifty-seven and beginning that waking-up stage that I spoke about in Chapter 1. There had to be more for me to do in this life. Even my boss told me that I was overqualified for this position and that I had way more talent than I was using in this job.

This is when I made that choice that I was going to find my true purpose and passion and figure out a way to do it. I didn't have any more time to lose. It was now or never.

I looked at options. I started following ideas, like learning to be a virtual assistant. I bought a book and started learning how to build a business as a VA. Not too far down that path, I realized that although I loved the idea of having my own home-based business working my own hours and finding clients I wanted to work with, I was not excited about the work itself. I didn't enjoy it in our family fun center, and I was bored with it at the elementary school. So, I ditched that idea and kept searching. I finally committed to finding the thing that I was meant to do that would utilize my natural talents and strengths and be something I am deeply passionate about. I was not going to create just another job for myself. Never again!

My commitment to finding my passion and purpose led me to becoming a coach. That was *the* thing! How did I find it? I went on a self-discovery journey to get to know myself. I was in my late fifties, and it was dawning on me that I didn't truly know myself.

Do You Know Who You Truly Are?

Many of us are going through life believing we are someone else because we don't know our identity. We take on the identity that someone else has given us or that we give ourselves because we haven't taken the time to discover who we really are. We are living out of those false inner stories I talked about in Chapter 7. But when we become who we truly are, our entire being will shine forth in our unique and authentic colors (and we may even look younger, too).

You are so unique. No one else on earth shares your DNA. Your fingerprints, your voice pattern, the number of the proteins in your hair and how they are arranged, and even your tongue print and skin tone are all unique features of your being. Your uniqueness goes deeper than the physical body you inhabit, however. How you think, how you view the world and yourself, how you make decisions and interpret what's going on around you, how you communicate, how you interact with others, and how you express yourself also make you unique. Your natural abilities and tendencies, innate gifts and talents, experiences, upbringing, education, and perspective all make up who you are.

We can think we are someone else other than who we truly are. I recently had a color analysis done. A color analysis is usually done by an image consultant. They identify the best colors for your skin, hair, and eye color so that when you shop for clothes, accessories, and cosmetics, you can find them in the colors that look best on you. This particular company categorizes your colors into the names of the seasons. I discovered that I was a Fall, not a Winter. Years ago, when having your "colors done" became popular, I was told that I was a Winter. For the last forty years, I have worn Winter colors. They looked good on me, but my true colors make me look vibrant. Many women, just like me, spend years not knowing their true colors or their true selves. It not only takes time, but it also takes intention and effort to get to know yourself.

Why Is It So Important to Know Yourself?

The relationship you have with yourself is the most important one you'll ever have. You are with you twenty-four hours a day, seven days a week. If you don't know yourself, how will others know the real you? If you don't know yourself, then you are more than likely putting on another identity, like wearing the wrong colors. You'll try to be what others think you should be or what others expect you to be. If you let them, others will try to put another identity on you. They will try to get you to wear the wrong colors.

We don't know ourselves like we know others, and how ironic is that? How comfortable are you being alone with your thoughts, with nothing to distract you? When we don't feel comfortable with who we are, we begin to doubt, become more self-critical, rely on others' opinions, and compare ourselves with others. Then we believe those opinions are true because we haven't formed our own belief and knowledge of our true selves as our foundation.

Building a positive and loving relationship with yourself takes time, but it brings incredible freedom and joy. Being comfortable in your skin leads to happiness and a fulfilling life. Having that healthy, loving relationship helps to have empathy and compassion for yourself. You stop being your own worst critic.

Accept and embrace who you are. It positions you behind the steering wheel of your life. You take ownership. You step into your power.

FIVE NON-NEGOTIABLE DISCOVERIES YOU MUST MAKE ABOUT WHO YOU ARE

1. **Identify your dreams.** What did you dream of doing when you were a child? What would be your dream job, career, business, and life?

2. **Identify your passions.** What fires you up? What are the causes you willingly invest time, energy, and money in? What are your soapbox issues?

3. **Identify your core values.** What is most important to you? What drives your decisions? What must you have in your life that feels out of alignment when you aren't walking your talk?

4. **Identify your key strengths and talents.** What comes easily for you? What were you naturally good at and could do for hours and hours on end?

5. **Identify your personality.** There are lots of personality assessments out there, but I like to use the Enneagram assessment with my clients.

For me, it started with uncovering my innate strengths, personality, dreams, values, and passions. I shed the roles that did not fit me, and I found me. The turning point came when I took a strengths assessment that gave me deep insight into who I am. It was like turning on a light bulb in a dark room. I began to understand my natural, innate tendencies. I discovered that the reason I enjoyed parts of my job at the fun center and earlier as a teacher was because they were directly connected to my innate strengths.

Why is it so important to identify your talents and strengths and build on them to bring your dreams into reality?

In 1998, Tom Rath began working with a team of scientists from Gallup, led by the late Donald O. Clifton, known as the Father of Strengths Psychology. Based on a forty-year study of human strengths, they developed language around the thirty-four most common talents they identified in people. An assessment called the StrengthsFinder (now called Clifton Strengths) was created to help people discover these talents. Through this research, they discovered that the people who are most satisfied and successful in life spend most of their time and energy developing and growing their talents, their natural strengths, rather than focusing on weaker areas. You'll perform better, build an exceptional level of skill, and you'll be happier and more satisfied. People who try to improve areas where they are not naturally gifted usually struggle, and even though they can build a high level of skill in those areas through hard work and practice, they are not able to reach their highest potential, achieve their highest goals, and do not experience the deepest satisfaction in life.

The Gallup research revealed that "people who do have the opportunity to focus on their strengths every day are six times more likely to be engaged in their jobs and three times as likely to report having an excellent quality of life in general."[24]

Unfortunately, we are influenced by our education and culture to focus more on our weak areas to make them stronger. However, as the Gallup research has shown, this doesn't work. A person who struggles with math isn't likely to become an accomplished accountant or statistician. The good news is that even though there are areas where we are weak, we each have great potential in our innate areas of talent. When we build on those specific areas, we are developing who we already are. That is where our greatness lies. When we focus on building those areas, we have the potential to excel at the highest levels and enjoy deep satisfaction and fulfillment.

Gallup researched almost every major culture, country, industry, and position and found that "a strengths-based approach improves your confidence, direction, hope, and kindness toward others."[25]

Why isn't everyone focusing on developing and growing in their areas of strength?

They don't know what their innate talents are. They can't describe them to you. Most women will tell me they have no idea what their areas of strength are, but they can quickly list all their areas of weakness. Why? We grew up that way. Gallup's research showed that the majority of parents in cultures worldwide believe that the lowest grades needed the most attention instead of investing in areas of strength where our greatest potential lies. It's no wonder we have such difficulty identifying our strengths.

One of my top talent themes that showed up in the Clifton Strengths Assessment is called Developer. For me, this means that I have the innate ability to see potential in others and help them develop it. I am exceptionally good at creating paths of learning that allow them to make progress in incremental steps, and I champion each small step with them. My strength lies in this step-by-step growth and progress and being able to guide, teach, and mentor them until they are successful. This one insight revealed the reasons why I loved teaching school and developing my staff at the fun center. Teaching and managing were the channels through which my true gift could be expressed so that what I did flowed from who I am. It isn't being a teacher, manager, or coach that defines me. Those are merely roles through which my true self found its highest meaning and expression when those roles drew from my greatest strengths.

The authors of the book *Life Keys: Discover Who You Are* call this knowing your "life gifts." These life gifts express themselves in various ways throughout your life, such as the ability to communicate well, solve problems, analyze situations, activate others to complete a project, or create a beautiful piece of art or a natural sense of rhythm in music. When you develop those areas of your life gifts, you have the most optimal opportunity to feel deep satisfaction and fulfillment in your life.

"A root source of satisfaction in life is doing what comes naturally—using your own unique blend of life gifts. Things that seem so easy for you that you assume anyone could do them may, in fact, be your life gifts."[26]

When I was young, I started a little neighborhood school in my basement. I invited the neighbor kids over and sat them down at their desks, and I would teach them. But this was not a game to me. I wanted to teach them something new—expand their knowledge. I would find out what they knew and then I would come up with a way to add to that knowledge. If they knew how to add, I would teach them subtraction. The amazing thing was that even after going to school all day, they would still come over to my "school" and do whatever I asked them to do. I loved it so much. I was naturally good at explaining new concepts to each child so that they could grasp what I was teaching them. I saw the potential in them, and I knew how to draw it out of them. It excited and thrilled me to see growth, to see the light come on in their eyes when they understood it. This wasn't difficult. I didn't struggle to do it. For me, it was fascinating and so much fun. This was a clue to my core strengths and natural talent.

I pursued the passion for teaching and built on that natural ability through my first career as a teacher. I loved it and felt fulfilled and satisfied for many years. And then I didn't. There came a time when I no longer wanted to teach. I felt burned out and drained. That's when I resigned from teaching and began the family fun center with my husband. Did that mean that I had wasted my time all those years teaching? No, it meant that I entered a new season as my purpose continued to unfold. Was running the family fun center business, or working as an office manager a mistake or a waste of time? Absolutely not! I learned even more about myself through those roles and developed my potential and skills that I now use in growing my coaching business. They were crucial components of my development and growth in fulfilling my ultimate purpose in life.

Suzanne was shocked to discover one of her talents when she took the CliftonStrengths Assessment. This talent, called Restorative, enables her to be a problem-solver. This is something she never considered as one of her strengths. But as we explored further, she realized that she is. She took notice about how she operates at work, including her ability to notice deficiencies in processes, seeing what needs to be improved and changed. This comes to her easily and naturally, and it shows up at work and home. She finds herself rearranging things to work better, trying new things, and making improvements so that things go more smoothly.

Suzanne was also amazed to discover that what her husband notes as her tendency to "mull" over things is a natural talent. It shows up in her slowness at making decisions, not because she is indecisive, but because she naturally deliberates and thoroughly considers every aspect of the decision. She sets high standards for herself, more stringent and detailed standards than others would set for her. She once thought this was a weakness, but through this self-discovery process, she came to embrace her deliberative talent as a huge asset. Through this strength, she can see what others miss, and she creates amazing solutions for complex problems or processes in her personal life as well as her winemaking business.

Another revelation for Suzanne was the delightful discovery that her insatiable desire to learn is a gift and a strength. Instead of trying to resist this desire, thinking that it is frivolous and a foolish use of time, energy, and finances, she embraced it, understanding that her love of learning, studying, taking notes, and mastering skills is a talent she can build on to become successful and masterful as a winemaker. She only needed to channel this love for learning into a specific path of professional development that eventually will lead her to achieve her long-term goals. She could completely submerge herself in her studies and embrace the learning process because she released any guilt associated with investing resources in her learning. She gave herself permission to be who she is and to do what she loves.

Suzanne noticed her confidence growing as she understood and embraced her innate talents. She felt clearer in the direction she wanted to take her life and energized and motivated because she was igniting her passions. She is more assured about the decisions she is making. She is showing up differently in her life—more engaged, present, and calm. Her stress levels have been reduced significantly.

Suzanne is a perfect example of how impactful this self-discovery work can be in a person's life. As you uncover your unique design, you can embrace the greatness you see inside yourself. This is the most important aspect of realizing your purpose.

Your Purpose Unfolds Throughout Life

Christian coach and author Tony Stoltzfus says, "Purpose is implanted in us as well as revealed to us—we were made for what God calls us to be."[27]

One thing I have come to understand is that life's purpose is not something we find and then we have it and that's it. As we have experiences, our purpose reveals itself. Some things that we do feel like flow—like we are in the zone. Everything is effortless and timeless, and we are so engaged in the activity that we've lost track of everything else. We feel satisfied and fulfilled and can't wait to do it again. Those experiences give us clues about our purpose and our inner design, what we were uniquely suited to do and to be.

Other things that we do will feel like work. We feel drained and depleted, even if the outcome was successful. These experiences give us clues about what are not our strengths. The point is that we learn from all our experiences, and all that we learn, we can bring to the table as we sharpen our understanding of the fullness of our life purpose.

It's a journey of self-discovery, growth, and the ripening of wisdom. I think it's meant to be that way, and I don't believe you can rush the process. If you try to rush through it, you only slow it down. You become more of who you already are as you journey through life. Purpose is not a destination; it's a becoming, "a dynamic, adaptive journey" as Tony Stoltzfus said. "Seeing the heart of life purpose as an incarnation you become, instead of a mission you do, can make an enormous difference in the trajectory of your life."[28]

Stoltzfus talks about the idea of convergence when you reach your midlife years. This is the idea that in the later seasons of life, when your stages of preparation and career-building are complete, you move into a place of purpose fulfillment rather than discovery, preparation, growth, and learning. This often begins in your fifties and sixties when there is a growing desire to make an impact, to mentor and impart wisdom to others, and to leave a legacy. It's a sense of the fulfillment of one's life mission through a culmination of all that has emerged through the journey of life. What you have experienced, the knowledge you have cultivated, the skills you have honed, and the wisdom you have developed throughout your life converge into this purpose-fulfillment space.

This means that nothing has been wasted or lost. You haven't wasted time on anything you've done or experienced in your life because it all contributes to this convergence, and it is all for a reason and part of your life purpose of becoming the fullest version of you.

This is extremely good news!

Five Roadblocks to Discovering Your Greatness

1. **Concern about others' opinions.** One roadblock I discovered as I began this journey was worrying about what others would think of what I can do or not do. Or what they think I "should" do. If I venture out to do something new and start a business "at my age," friends and family could get upset with me or be worried that I'm taking too big of a risk and I might fail. Even the thought of this can stop you because you feel guilty and unsure of yourself. I needed an unshakable belief in myself and in my ability to work hard and learn what I need to learn to create this new life for myself. I had to see how great I really am!

   Roy T. Bennett, author of *The Light in the Heart*, wrote, "Don't let the expectations and opinions of other people affect your decisions. It's your life, not theirs. Do what matters most to you; do what makes you feel alive and happy. Don't let the expectations and ideas of others limit who you are. If you let others tell you who you are, you are living their reality—not yours."[29]

2. **It's too late/I'm too old.** Another roadblock that can pop up in this journey is the belief that it's too late or we're too old to pursue those passions and dreams from our youth. They've been on the shelf lying dormant for so long. Thoughts like "that ship has sailed" or "it's too late for me to pursue that." Challenge those thoughts with "Why not? I'm still alive and kicking!"

After examining the lives of hundreds of historical, biblical, and contemporary leaders, Dr. J. Robert Clinton gained perspective on how leaders develop over a lifetime. In his book, *The Making of a Leader: Recognizing the Lessons and Stages of Leadership Development*, he identified six distinct stages of how leaders develop over their lifetime. In the last two stages, he describes the idea of "convergence." This is the season of life where your "gift-mix" and your experiences over your lifetime merge into a place of maturity and fulfillment of your life's calling and mission. Far from being a time when your gifts are no longer needed, you are in a season when your gifts, wisdom, knowledge, and passion to serve and make an impact are essential and needed by those around you. This is the season of life to step up even more fully into your dreams and passions.[30]

The ability to function in your strengths is also a function of your life stage. People from their forties to sixties have reached a stage of maximum productivity. They are more aware and in tune with their purpose in life and are at a place where they're ready to fully step into it. In their younger years, they're still learning, skill-building, and experiencing things that are preparing them for the fulfillment of purpose.

In your midlife years, you're at a place of finding that "best-fit" role in life where you can maximize your impact. You are at a place in your life where years of experiences, knowledge, skills, wisdom, and character development converge in the most amazing season of life you've ever had before.

3. **Inaction.** The truth is that you have infinite potential inside of you in the form of seeds. But that potential does not become reality without action on your part. This is where many people get stuck. We all would like to have our dreams come true and reach our fullest potential without having to do anything to make them happen. It would be great if all that we desire would just pop up in front of us, but that is not how it works.

Steve Maraboli said, "Potential remains an intangible possibility until you participate; until you ACT. You are the activator that bridges potentiality and reality. You are the point of origin for things to transcend from the realm of the possible to the tangible. Take action toward the life you desire. When we do not act, potentiality becomes the soil that houses the seeds of your regret."[31]

The secret is knowing that it's the small steps that get you there. One small step at a time will yield major changes and results. How does a mountain climber scale Mount Everest? One step at a time.

The power of the small steps cannot be overestimated. Once you take that first small step, you feel great that you've made progress, and that inspires and motivates you to take the next small step. Before you know it, you're well on your way. Take that mountain and break it down into smaller milestones, like base camps on the way up the mountain. Then focus on taking only the steps you need to take to get to that base camp. Soon, you'll be on top of the mountain.

Steve Maraboli also said, "It is easy to be discouraged at the mountain of change we seek in our lives. At the same time, it's important to remember that the mountain of change, just like an actual mountain, can only be scaled one step at a time."[32]

4. **It's difficult to believe in yourself.** What are the words you speak over yourself? What do you call yourself? What do you say to your reflection when looking in a mirror? Words matter. They can have a powerful and lasting impact on our minds, our emotions, and our hearts. They can make a deep impression on how we define ourselves and the life that we create.

Just as words can have a powerful negative impact on our lives, the opposite is also true. Words that speak to our true selves, that call to the greatness inside each one of us, also have a powerful impact. They will propel us forward and help us fully walk in who we were meant to be.

Wayne Dyer said, "If you change the way you look at things, the things you look at will change." This is also true about who you are. If you change the way you see yourself, you will change and become your true self.

That is what I set out to do. I changed the words I spoke into my life and over my life. My words were in harmony with what I was discovering about who I am. Instead of saying, I'm too old or I don't know how, I started saying, "I'm never too old as long as I'm alive and still have breath in me. I'll pursue my passions. I'll learn whatever I need to learn. I'll do whatever it takes."

Instead of worrying about what I didn't have, I started saying, "I am blessed. I have more than I need. I'm attracting abundance into my life. I'm attracting the people who I need to know and learn from. I'm attracting my ideal clients."

Instead of wondering who would want to read my book, I started saying, "My book is a gift to the world. No one else can write this book because no one else is me."

I began to speak a new name over myself. Names we have been given and names we call ourselves carry a huge impact. A name is significant. In my journal entry that I shared at the beginning of this chapter, I wrote, "It's important to know the name I've given you because it describes what I have woven into your DNA—your nature and your character."

I could give myself these new names because that is who I am. I knew who I was because I did the self-discovery work to find out who I have been uniquely designed by God to be. Now I could believe in myself with full assurance in my worth and value. I could see the greatness God had placed within me. Words have power, but their power comes from what you believe is true about them.

Stasi Eldridge said, "There is power in what we name ourselves. There is power in what other people name us as well. Both the power to bless and the power to curse come from the heart and flow out of the mouth through words. What we call something, what we are called, whether good or evil, will play itself out in our lives."[33]

You become who you truly are when you see your worth and value as a human on this planet. The key is to discover your true greatness and all the brilliance and beauty and strength that is uniquely you. The key is to root out the source of the thoughts holding you back, those old squatters on your estate, and replace them with thoughts rooted in truth.

Thoughts of doubt and fear can never accomplish anything. They always lead to failure. Strong thoughts with purpose and energy and the power to do and to be will cease when doubt and fear creep in. That's when you put the brakes on your life, and you stay in your comfort zone and settle for less than who you were meant to be. Your actions spring from your thoughts. Don't hope you prove yourself wrong. Take action to prove yourself right. When you find yourself hiding behind a mask and staying in your comfort zone, then think about what you're thinking about. Change the narrative.

What are the words you are speaking to your heart? What do you believe is true about who you are? No one in this world can be you, except you. If you're trying to be someone else to please others, you are wearing a mask. People can sense when you're wearing a mask and not being genuine, which can lead to rejection, that thing you fear. People are attracted to the real thing. People will accept you more even if you're quirky or different if you are being the real you. When you show up authentic, you create the space for others to do the same.

Oscar Wilde said, "Be yourself. Everyone else is taken."

Authenticity is being confident enough to walk away from places and situations where you can't be yourself, choosing the places and relationships that allow you to be you. Be more concerned with truth than opinions. Be who you are unapologetically. Be vulnerable without fear. Be awake to your feelings and desires. Be free from others' opinions. Believe in yourself!

5. **You lack support**. We are wired for connection. Every human on the planet longs to know that they belong. Discovering your unique greatness requires you to surround yourself with people who see that greatness in you and call it out of you. We were not meant to walk this life on our own. We need community. We need our tribe, our circle, our support group.

Brené Brown said, "True belonging is the spiritual practice of believing in and belonging to yourself so deeply that you can share your most authentic self with the world and find sacredness in both being a part of something and standing alone in the wilderness. True belonging doesn't require you to change who you are; it requires you to be who you are."[34]

This is vitally important to remember when you are looking for that community. If you don't know who you are first and if you're not being your most authentic self, you will not find your true tribe. You will easily fall into the trap of trying to please others so that you fit in. But when you know who you are and you belong to yourself deeply, as Brown said, you will find your true tribe. You will belong, and you will experience the strong foundation of support that you need to thrive and allow your greatness to be expressed to the world.

"*Spirituality is recognizing and celebrating that we are all inextricably connected by a power greater than all of us and that our connection to that power and to one another is grounded in love and compassion. Practicing spirituality brings a sense of perspective, meaning, and purpose to our lives.*"[35]

When you understand that we are connected in a deeply spiritual way, then you begin to understand how much we need to find our community. This can be a small circle of close friends, family, or even a mastermind or networking group where you can find that connection around your business or professional growth. We need our spiritual tribe, too, our faith community as well as family and friends.

These connections and deep relationships help us grow to our fullest potential. They help us believe in ourselves so we can grow deep roots and thrive. We also need to support others and help them grow.

Loneliness is one of the most common experiences on the planet, and it is not a good feeling. There's a reason for that. Studies on loneliness have shown that when we feel isolated and disconnected, we try to protect ourselves, and we can spiral downward into a state of defensiveness, less empathy, and fearfulness. We create even more stories about what others think of us, and we can be covered in shame, thinking that we don't belong and are unworthy of love. This is a dangerous, unhealthy state to be in.

When you feel lonely, that is a warning sign that you need to reach out, not isolate. The answer is not in joining a bunch of random groups in a desperate attempt to fit in. Studies have also shown that it is the quality of relationships that matters, not the quantity.[36]

I have felt lonely many times. It hurts deeply. I start making up stories about myself when I feel lonely. I start accusing others for my loneliness, and it's easy to feel unwanted because people aren't coming to *me*. When you start making up stories like that, especially with words like *never* and *no one*, stop that narrative and question the truth of it.

It goes like this for me: "Never? Really? Is that true? What about that invite you got a week ago to join your friends for a day at the lake? You turned it down, remember? Oh yeah, that's right. I chose not to go because I was tired."

Check those stories out. More often they are not true, or at least not entirely. Then ask yourself if you have reached out to anyone lately. The adage is true: if you want to have friends, be a friend. I have discovered that when I feel lonely, if I will call someone or invite someone to go for a hike or have lunch or meet me for dinner, they are grateful for the invitation. Often, they have been feeling lonely, too.

I wrote about loneliness in one of my speeches:

"Loneliness is the worst feeling ever. It cuts so deep that it can literally take your breath away. All of us were born with a need for connection and belonging. It's hardwired into the fabric of our being. It's almost as powerful as the need to breathe. Feeling like you don't belong, or you're not wanted slices like a knife into your core.

This is my private pain. I have felt the pain of loneliness often, but I don't speak of it. People don't know this about me.

How can you talk about it? You either sound pitiful and needy, which makes others feel uncomfortable, or you sound mean and desperate, and then people tell you it's your fault. I haven't spoken about it. I just suffer in silence, watching while others get invited to parties and events, even going on vacation together while I do most things alone. I sit alone at church, I go to movies alone, and I go dancing and biking and walking—alone.

But I don't want you to feel sorry for me right now because I've learned a powerful truth in my struggle with loneliness. I've learned that although I may at times feel the pain of loneliness, I'm never alone. While you've been listening to me, you've probably thought that I could be talking about you. This is your story, too. We all struggle with loneliness. We all at some time or another have felt rejected and left out.

The powerful truth that I've learned is that loneliness is a lie. Not being chosen is a lie. We've all been chosen. Every single one of us was chosen to be exactly who we are. Jesus even said so in the Bible. He said, "I have chosen you."

We were all created with a need for connection and belonging because we are chosen, and we do belong. What I've realized is that when I feel the sting of rejection from others, it has nothing to do with me, with my worthiness to be loved, with my value, or with who I am.

It has everything to do with the other person's pain. I've realized that when I sit at home feeling lonely, wondering why I wasn't invited, the people I want to invite me are also sitting at home feeling lonely and uninvited. They are also wondering why they haven't been chosen. They are also feeling the pain of loneliness. I am not alone in this.

I've learned that when I embrace the truth that I am chosen, I am empowered to choose myself. When I stand in the truth of my own worthiness and belonging, I become my own best friend.

When I stand in this place of self-love and self-acceptance and see that I've been placed here on this earth on purpose because I am chosen to be me, then I am centered in love. I become like a tree that bears much fruit. The fruit of my life then becomes attractive and endearing to others. When I stand in my truth, I am strong, and I am full, and I can pour out from that fullness to others. When I reject the lie of not being chosen, I find that I am invited. An email comes that asks if I want to have coffee. A friend calls and says let's go dancing or to the movies. It happens as naturally as it was meant to happen. Whenever loneliness tries to creep back into my heart, all I need to do is to stand in my truth: I am chosen. I do belong."

You Belong and You Are Worthy of Love

Choose yourself. Choose to show up with authenticity, embracing your greatness and your worthiness. Be your own best friend first. Belong to yourself first, then you can reach out to others and make deep connections with those people who want to be with you—your tribe. They are out there, and you will find them, I promise.

I recommend taking a few assessments to discover your innate strengths and unique personality traits. I often use these types of assessments with my coaching clients and in my programs.

You'll find an exercise in the STAR Guide to get you started: My Self-Discovery Sheet.

Then you can move on to pursuing your passions!

Access the Digital Workbook: https://bit.ly/StarGuideWorkbook or the Paperback Workbook: https://amzn.to/3JUkchQ

CHAPTER 9

PURSUE YOUR PASSIONS

Without the dynamism of passion, we never engage our life mission with the drive and enthusiasm necessary to pull it off.[37]

~Tony Stoltzfus

Wherefore I put thee in remembrance that thou stir up the gift of God, which is in thee by the putting on of my hands. For God hath not given us the spirit of fear; but of power, and of love, and of a sound mind.

~2 Timothy 1:67

FROM MY JOURNAL (AGE 50)

Right now, my life is in a place of total change. I have no idea what to do as far as a job. I feel such a surge of expectancy and confidence that I haven't felt in a long time. I feel like I'm being called to go out on the water where nothing is certain and there's risk and a big unknown, but somehow, I feel that's the safest place to be because it's where God is calling me right now. I need to trust Him and this intuitive pulling in my heart. This is scary! I believe that's what the Lord is bringing me into in this next season of my life. I don't know what this will look like or what I'll be doing, exactly, but I do know it's a new direction for me.

TRUST THE PULL OF YOUR HEART

Have you ever felt that invisible pull toward something? A stirring inside that feels exciting and full of possibility? Those are the embers of passion and purpose igniting in your soul.

Without passion and purpose, you are just getting through life, living for the weekend or vacations. That's no way to live. We are wired for this—to long for a purpose. But it is rarely something that manifests itself easily. It always requires a search.

Have you ever watched the Olympics? I'm always amazed by the incredible things these athletes can do. I know a woman in her sixties who competes in 100-mile races. Can you imagine running for one hundred miles? I can't even run for one mile without being winded. I told her that I could never do that, and she said, "Yes you could, if you trained. You can do anything you want to do!"

Of course, she is right. If I wanted to become an ultra-runner or an ultra-athlete, I could get into a training regimen, and if I were committed to it and diligent, I could eventually run 100-mile races. But I don't have the drive or desire to become an ultra-runner. No interest whatsoever.

So, what is it that makes my friend, and those Olympic athletes, endure hours upon hours of training and hard work through blood, sweat, and tears? How do they keep going even when they're exhausted and in pain? What kept Mother Theresa working for a lifetime in the slums of Calcutta? What drives amazingly talented teachers to remain in inner-city schools amid drug- and gang-infested neighborhoods?

Passion—they are fueled by a burning passion for what they do.

Passion fills you with the enthusiasm, focus, and energy to pursue something until you succeed. When you love what you are doing, it fulfills you, and your passion for it will keep you going even in the face of obstacles, failures, and hard work. When you have passion for your purpose, you won't give up. You'll persevere until you succeed. And you keep going.

Have you ever gotten so involved in something that hours passed by as if they were minutes? And then when you were finished, you couldn't wait to do it again even if you were exhausted and even if you ran into difficulties along the way? That's passion.

Is This All There Is?

A client confessed to me that she was feeling tormented by this thought: is this all there is? Ever feel that way? You watch a movie or read a book, and at the end, you feel like there should have been more. What about at the end of a vacation? Or even in your relationships? How about with your life?

This is a common experience in the midlife years. That's where the "midlife crisis" idea originated. Suddenly, people wake up and realize life is going by fast, and they feel like they are missing out on something. There must be more.

Let's break this down a bit to understand what is going on.

Why Do We Feel This Vague Sense of Dissatisfaction with Our Lives?

Part of it comes from the "waiting to be happy" syndrome. When this happens, I'll be happy. When I get this or that, when I land that job or get that promotion, when I get that house, then I'll be happy. You get the idea. Of course, this can happen at any stage of life, but it becomes sharply focused during the midlife season. As we age, we realize that fulfilling our mission in this life is determined by the choices we make. Life is short. The time to act is now.

How do people create happiness? What happens in our brains when we are happy instead of depressed? Happiness researchers have found that "waiting to be happy" limits our brain's potential for success and our capacity for feeling fulfilled and satisfied with life. On the other hand, when we cultivate a positive mindset, we are more motivated, efficient, resilient, creative, and productive—which then creates success and satisfaction.[38]

The key word in what I just said is *cultivate*.

Yes, that's right. It's up to you to cultivate a positive outlook and create happiness in your life. Happiness doesn't just come to you if you do all the right things. You create a positive mindset and cultivate happiness, then success in all aspects of your life will follow. We've had it backward.

How do you define happiness? You are the best judge of how happy you are. It's based on how we feel about our lives. Scientists define happiness as the experience of positive emotions—pleasure combined with deeper feelings of meaning and purpose. Happiness implies a positive mood in the present and a positive outlook for the future.

So, if you're asking yourself "Is this all there is?" every day, you are probably not experiencing happiness consistently, and you may need to dive deeper to discover your passions.

It Always Goes Back to Your "Why"

Someone asked me once how it is that I can keep on building my business even when it looks like nothing is happening, and nothing seems to be working.

Such a great question!

My short answer was that I always go back to my "why." Why am I doing what I'm doing? What is my motivation for creating this business? What is the passion behind it that drives me to keep going and not give up, no matter what? My passion gives me my "why," and that creates crazy motivation to get up every day and keep at it. Keep building and creating, keep reaching out to women, keep talking and sharing what I bring to the world. Passion fuels the fire and creates motivation.

The reason you do anything is driven by what motivates you to do it. You can be motivated by things internally or externally, and sometimes what is motivating you is not all that positive or sustainable. If you want to stay the course with anything you are doing and achieve the desired results, then it is important to understand what is driving you.

So often, I've heard women say, "I just can't find it! I still don't know what my passion is." Many women wrestle with this feeling. It seems so evasive and always just out of reach. There are a myriad of people sharing ideas about how to find your passion. Search "how to find your passion," and you'll come up with a long list of articles with endless tips and keys to help you. But somehow people still struggle to nail down their passions.

So, if everyone is looking for their passion, and there are tons of people telling you how to find it, why haven't we all found it by now? Why is it so hard to find?

I have a theory about that. My theory is based on one core idea: we're looking in the wrong place.

My Three Discoveries About Finding Your Passion

As I ventured out on that water to explore and discover my passion and purpose, I began to discover three emerging themes: there is a River of Passion, a Fire of Passion, and a Pain of Passion.

The River of Passion: It is not something you find, like at the end of the rainbow. You haven't lost your passions somewhere along the way so that now you need to find them. They've always been with you. They have grown and evolved along with you. You can't find your passions by thinking about them. Passions live in your heart, not your head.

Passions live underneath what you are doing. They go deep, like an underground river flowing through your life. They show up when you are moving and doing, immersing yourself in wholehearted living. They are like an underground force of nature, spurring you on, driving you to keep exploring and expanding.

As I shared in a previous chapter, my childhood passion was teaching. When I played with my dolls, they would always be sitting in a classroom with me as the teacher. I started a "school" in my basement, inviting the neighborhood kids to come. I was not satisfied to play school. I wanted to teach them something new. As an adult, I became a teacher and taught for twenty years. I always thought that my passion was teaching, but now I believe that my true passion ran much deeper.

Teaching in elementary school was the vehicle that carried and released my deeper passions. Passions are not necessarily what we *do*. Teaching is a gift, a strength, an innate ability, but teaching by itself is not my passion. The passion that compelled me to teach is an intense desire to help people walk fully in their true potential. That is the underground river that has flowed through my entire life.

The Fire of Passion: I always got fired up when my students learned something. When the light went on in their eyes, and they knew they got it. When they grew a little bit more confident in themselves and their value, I was more motivated to be the best teacher I could. It compelled me to spend hours on lessons, grading papers, and setting up my classroom. I didn't like the grading and lesson planning, but I was willing to endure it so that I could satisfy my passion for helping others grow.

I like the Urban Dictionary's definition of passion: "Passion is when you put more energy into something than is required to do it. It is more than just enthusiasm or excitement, passion is the ambition that is materialized into action to put as much heart, mind, body, and soul into something as is possible."[39]

Other definitions describe passion as a strong and barely controllable emotion, intense, driving, or overmastering feeling or conviction. Synonyms for passion are fervor, ardor, enthusiasm, and zeal. These are intense emotions that compel you to action. Passion is an emotion that deeply stirs your soul.

When I discovered life coaching, it was as if smoldering embers had been stirred up inside my soul and ignited into a flame. I was stoked after every coaching session. Seeing a person's eyes when they discovered the possibilities inside of them ignites intense emotion in me and I get fired up. This is what compelled me to become a teacher and then later to become a coach. The passion is the same, the container changed.

Ask yourself why you are fired up—why something is so important to you that you feel that intense emotion compelling you to action; you'll find your passion. But there is another aspect to passion that many people overlook—and that is the Pain of Passion.

The Pain of Passion: The origin of the word *passion* carries the meaning "to suffer." The passion of Christ refers to His suffering and death on the cross.[40]

Look to your pain to discover your passions. Pay close attention to your greatest struggles and trials. What emerges out of the battles you have fought and the hard work and pain you have willingly endured?

Often, it is in your greatest struggles that your passions are refined and strengthened. My greatest sufferings have come from being a woman and being used, manipulated, held back, and exploited simply because I was a woman. Because of what I have suffered, my passion for helping people realize their fullest potential became more refined and focused on women. This is the soapbox on which I could preach endlessly. Women have been held back and told to stay in the background for far too long. My passion now is to empower them to walk boldly in who they are and never let the world tell them they can't.

If you look deeply enough, you'll see that your passion is what keeps you going even when you're exhausted. You'll keep fighting even when you're under attack. You are willing to suffer loss and hardship and go through intense struggles when you are passionate about something.

Passions will drive you to find ways around, through, or over obstacles. If you're not passionate about something, obstacles will stop you. The stronger your passion is, the more determined you will be when you encounter obstacles. Nothing could stop me from being a coach and working hard and long hours to create a business that empowers women. I don't mind the struggle or the hard work. I hardly even notice it.

Your greatest struggles and trials can provide clues to your passions. They can also be the furnace that forges your greatest desires. What are the things you are willing to suffer hardship to obtain?

Tina is a woman who wrestled with inner passions that did not match her outer circumstances. She was working a job that did not fulfill her. Inside, she yearned for a better quality of life. She longed to be someone who wakes up every day not dreading going to work, not having to always rush, and not living under the pressure to be someone she's not. Tina's burning passion was to connect with others and make a difference. She wanted to be a coach or a counselor—to be in a helping profession where she could pour into others in a way that helped them live their best lives, too.

With tears streaming down her face, Tina expressed her anguish. She was losing herself. She felt heavy, weighed down, like she was underwater with her feet tied to concrete blocks. Her jaws were tight. Her feet felt numb, and her body felt clammy. The message she heard in her heart was "How could you let yourself get here?"

She felt deep disappointment with herself. She had not followed her heart, and she beat herself up for settling for less than what she truly desired. Yet, as we worked together, a beautiful truth emerged from her heart. She began to talk about how often the people she worked with would come to her for a listening ear and a safe place to let out their frustrations. People came to her for advice and help all the time.

When she realized this, her heart was filled with hope. Tina was able to explore deeper, underneath the pain and struggle she was feeling. She discovered something amazing. Although she wasn't working in a job that fulfilled her, her passion to help others still flowed like a river beneath her circumstances. She embraced the truth that she was already walking in the role of a counselor and a coach because this was her natural strength. She flowed in it even while working a day job. Tina realized that all her life, she had been making a difference in people's lives in this way. In the light of this emerging realization, she was able to stop beating herself up and to see her present job as a place along her journey, not the destination.

As she practiced self-compassion and accepted herself as she was and where she was in her journey, Tina was energized and motivated to unchain her feet from those concrete blocks by changing her story from "How could you let yourself get here?" to "Where do I want to go now and what is my first step?" She threw off the weight of that victim mentality and allowed her pain and struggle to teach her more about herself. She made the choice to honor that, created a plan of action, and took the first step toward getting her counseling degree. Tina enrolled in a counseling program and is now bringing her passion and her dream together. She is on her way to fulfilling her purpose.

The process of pursuing your passions will transform you into the person you are meant to be. Our life purpose is about becoming who we are, not just doing things. Becoming who you are will enable you to make your dreams a reality. Obstacles are the training ground of your calling.

There are lessons in our trials. Looking at struggle and suffering through this lens will change the experience.

Consider these questions to understand what your struggles are teaching you:

1. What is this struggle teaching me about my purpose?
2. What is so important in this endeavor that it keeps me going even when it hurts or is difficult?
3. What is this obstacle teaching me?

Why Is It So Difficult to Find Our Passions?

I think it's because they are there all along, and we've missed them because we are looking somewhere else. Your passions are there, underneath the surface. It's not about finding your passion as much as it is about uncovering the passion that is already there. You do that by looking at your heart, to that river flowing underneath all that you do, to the fire in your belly that gets stirred up about certain things, and to the pain you've endured without giving up.

If you look there, you'll find what you've never lost.

I completely resonate with what Tony Stoltzfus said about passion. "Passion is the underlying motivation and energy behind our life purpose. Our passions define what's most important to us, what we really care about, and what we energetically pursue. They are the urges that compel us to do something."[41]

Not too long ago, I traveled with my dad to Atlanta to see my youngest brother receive a prestigious award for his innovative approach to teaching biomedical engineering students. As I listened to my brother and two of his colleagues describe their work and share the history of how they got to where they are now, it struck me that underneath it all was this River of Passion that had fueled them even when faced with many obstacles. That passion flickered like a hot flame in their eyes and their voices at times during the presentation, and it seemed obvious to me that it was the driving force behind their success.

On the ride home, I asked my almost ninety-five-year-old father what jobs he had enjoyed most in his lifetime. He lit up, and energy infused his voice as he described them. The jobs he enjoyed the most were the ones where he was challenged to be innovative. He brought new solutions to complex problems in the world and took on positions where he could motivate and teach others to do the same. His favorite jobs were the ones that aligned most with his core passions. They had purpose and meaning to him.

Listen to Your Ninety-Five-Year-Old Self

Imagine you are ninety-five years old, sitting in your rocking chair, your family gathered around you. Someone asks you what your purpose in life was all about. What would you say? What do you want to be able to say?

You always have a choice. Imagine that at ninety-five, you will feel fully satisfied with your life. What would have had to happen for you to feel this way? What would you have accomplished? What difference would you have made in the world?

It comes down to you. You are the only one who can choose what you will do with your life.

It comes down to how you see yourself. Do you have a sense of your worth? As Robert S. McGee said, "A healthy self-concept is the recognition of one's value and worth: the understanding that as a unique human being, one has certain gifts and abilities unlike anyone else and can contribute to the world in a special way."[42]

This means that you believe in yourself. You can enjoy and value your strengths, talents, and passions. The things that come naturally to you do so easily and energize you. They are clues to help you find this sense of self-worth and the enjoyment of just being you.

Janet Attwood, co-author of *The Passion Test*, said, "Not one person on the planet is exactly like anyone else. You are unique. You have unique gifts that no one but you can give. You have those gifts because you have a special role to play in the world that requires giving those gifts. When you are playing that role, you are living your personal destiny. When you are aligned with your destiny, your life is joyful, delightful, exciting, and fulfilling. Your passions are the loves of your life. They are the things that are most deeply important to you. These are the things that, when you're doing them or talking about them, light you up."[43]

Take a moment to complete the *Passions Revealed* exercise in the **STAR Guide**.

We have arrived at the final phase of the STAR Process: Release the River.

Access the Digital Workbook: https://bit.ly/StarGuideWorkbook or the Paperback Workbook: https://amzn.to/3JUkchQ

PHASE FOUR:

RELEASE THE RIVER

Scan the QR Code above with your smartphone to view my Release the River message. Or follow this link:
https://youtu.be/0Uj8oJPCFXI

CHAPTER 10

DRAW FROM THE RIVER WITHIN

The endless and debilitating chatter in our minds often tries to talk us out of what our hearts are yearning to explore.

~ Marie Faleo

In the last day, that great day of the feast, Jesus stood and cried, saying, If any man thirst, let him come unto me, and drink. He that believeth on me, as the scripture hath said, out of his belly shall flow rivers of living water.

~ John 7:37-38

FROM MY JOURNAL (AGE 56)

Shine right where I've placed you. Yes, moment by moment and day by day. You are walking in your destiny as you abide in Me in each day and each moment. Tomorrow will take care of itself as you abide in Me today and right now in this moment. It's like a stream or channel. The water flows through the path laid out for it. It doesn't matter where or how other streams are flowing; your stream flows in the path I've ordained for you. Don't try to dig out your path or channel. That is My work. Just flow—let your spirit and soul flow in the path I have carved out for you, and don't worry about externals or others. What they think or say about you doesn't matter. I will make a way over, around, or through the obstacles the enemy or man may place in your path. My power at work within you is more than able to conquer obstacles and keep you moving in my path for you. So, just keep flowing, and take each day and moment as it comes, trusting Me that I am leading you in your destiny and purpose and in My plans for you.

YOU DRAW THE RIVER FROM INSIDE YOU, DON'T YOU?

This question was posed to me by a visiting minister preaching at my church six years before I wrote the journal entry above. I was stunned. I wasn't sure what he meant at first or why he asked me that question, but his eyes seemed to pierce like a laser beam into my soul. It landed in my heart and took root. It was to become a pivotal question in my life.

The preacher went on to say, "You've been through a rocky time. It's all been about attacking your confidence. The enemy knows that if he can make you insecure about your calling, you'll be ineffective. Your confidence must be in God alone. Be ready for changes!"

Little did I know how right he was. My life was about to go through major changes. Two months later, I was called into the pastor's office and told that several members of my worship team (I was the leader at the time) had called him with complaints. Remember the story I told you about in the chapter on forgiveness? This was that incident.

Drawing from the river inside me proved to be the single most powerful strategy I could ever have not only to survive that painful time, but to go on to a place on the other side of thriving, growing, and taking the center stage of my life with confidence in who I am. The river inside is where your power to live a fruitful, joyful life comes from. It's the river of your spirit, your perfect you, your best self. And it is where God's Spirit abides when you've received Him into your heart and life.

In John 7:37-39, Jesus proclaimed, *"If any man thirst, let him come unto me, and drink. He that believeth on me, as the scripture hath said, out of his belly shall flow rivers of living water. But this spake he of the Spirit, which they that believe on him should receive: for the Holy Ghost was not yet given, because that Jesus was not yet glorified."*

The very nature of rivers is to flow and move. They don't stay stagnant unless something is blocking their path. Rivers carry forward all that is within them and leave behind the debris that isn't needed or that doesn't serve the forward motion of the river as it rolls toward its destination. Rivers flow from their source to the ocean, and along the journey, they bring life and refresh all the living things they encounter.

When your life is in a state of flow from that river within, you will experience freedom and confidence. You will naturally release the wonderful gifts inside you with effortless power. The impact on those around you will be life changing. This is the goal of the **STAR Process**. This is when you will take center stage of your life as the star of your own story.

The river released from within you flows out to the waiting world. This is the fulfillment of your destiny. Just as rivers carve out a path and change the landscape wherever they flow, you will alter the atmosphere around you by being exactly who you are. There's nothing more powerful than a person who knows who they are, loves who they are, and releases their gifts to make the impact only they can make in the lives of others.

Just as the preacher told me, there would be big changes ahead. Life moves forward. Change is inevitable and a normal part of life. We must move with that flow. The journal message that opens this chapter came to me the day before my mom stepped into heaven. Her passing was unexpected and sudden. The day I wrote that entry, she was fine as far as I knew. My mom was being treated for a bladder infection that week, but it quickly escalated into pneumonia, and the infection overtook her body. Sepsis set in as she bled internally. Her brain hemorrhaged in the middle of the night. The next evening, with our family surrounding her hospital bed, the nurse turned off life support. We quickly realized that she had already left us hours earlier. We were devastated and heartbroken. Deep sorrow filled every nook and cranny of that room.

For the first time in decades, I allowed myself to feel the flood of emotions pouring through my mind, body, and heart. I let them come. I had come a long way on my journey to wholeness. I no longer feared the pain of strong emotions, and I drew from the river within for strength. I let the current carry me through the season of grief. It was a time of sorrow, but also of joy, knowing that my precious mom was dancing in heaven, completely released from all the restraints of her earthly life. We celebrated her life and the impact she had on so many people.

I drew comfort from the message I had received the day before. I took it moment by moment, abiding in the presence of God with me. I let my spirit and soul flow in the path carved out before me as Jesus led me, step by step and moment by moment, along my path of destiny.

Let's talk more about this concept of "when." When I get there, when I get my promotion, when I move, when I get that perfect job, when I get married, when the kids move out, when I reach this weight, when I do this, or when I do that . . . *then* I'll be a success. Then I'll be happy.

The problem with this mindset is that it creates uncertainty or a sense of lacking—it implies that something is missing now. It creates dissatisfaction and discontent. But when we embrace a path of mastery, we realize that there is no "there." A true master is always learning and growing and therefore, never arrives. It isn't even about arriving; it is about the process itself, the journey.

That's what releasing the river is all about. Rivers keep moving. They aren't stagnant. Every place the river touches is where it is in the moment and then it continues its journey. Rivers keep flowing until they reach the ocean. The same is true for us and our journey in life. We keep going, and each moment is where we are. Then we flow in our gifts and calling until we reach the end of our life here on earth, our ocean. Then we transition into eternity, carrying with us only what truly matters—fulfilling our true purpose during our lifetime on earth.

I believe in eternity. I believe we are eternal souls and that what we do with our time on earth will matter in eternity. Our lives make an impact here, but they also carry forward. So, looking through the lens of eternity, what would happen if you let go of the idea of "when I get there"?

What would your life look like if you stepped into the flow of your life now, in this moment, and released the river inside you, knowing the impact of your life will echo throughout all the ages?

How do you do that? Start by completing the *Release the River* exercise in the **STAR Guide**.

The next step in releasing the river within is to see clearly and engage fully.

Access the Digital Workbook: https://bit.ly/StarGuideWorkbook
or the Paperback Workbook: https://amzn.to/3JUkchQ

CHAPTER 11

CLEAR EYES, FULL HEART

Vision is the art of seeing what is invisible to others.

~Jonathan Swift

Brethren, I count not myself to have apprehended: but this one thing I do, forgetting those things which are behind, and reaching forth unto those things which are before, I press toward the mark for the prize of the high calling of God in Christ Jesus.

~Philippians 3:1314

FROM MY JOURNAL (AGE 66)

I see waves coming in toward me, one on top of the other. Some are small, some large. They are continuously rolling in. The water is clear and green, so beautiful and sparkling in the sunlight. A melody of joy rolls in on every wave.

Gifts hide within the waves underneath the breakers. In gratitude, I let the joy wash over me, breathing in the salty air, savoring the spray of water on my face and the warmth of each wave bathing my feet. As each wave subsides, I sink deeper into the soft sand, feeling increasingly grounded and secure.

The gifts begin to pile up on the shore around my feet and spread out far and wide. People come and gather the gifts. They open them with surprised delight. These gifts are not for me. They have come from my life as I have walked in my purpose. Saying yes to God has brought forth these gifts for others to receive. I am overwhelmed with joy, and I feel complete.

The Yo-Yo Syndrome

One of my new clients described her current situation to me the other day. She said that she will get an idea about what path she wants to take, and she'll get excited about it, but then another idea will come to her, and she'll think, "Maybe I should do that." It's like a yo-yo. She'll go back and forth from one idea to the next until she ends up in a pile of confusion. This is the reason she hired me. She has tried to figure it out on her own but has not been able to move forward.

This scenario is not unusual. I went through the same thing. It's not easy creating a clear path forward for yourself, and you can easily be pulled in one direction and then another until you feel lost in the woods.

I get it. I truly do. Circumstances of life beat us into submission—to settling and tolerating a ho-hum existence. We don't believe there is a way to have our dreams become reality. And maybe we try to pursue our dreams, but something goes wrong, we hit some obstacles, or our plans don't go anywhere, so eventually we just don't bother to dream anymore.

We give in to the idea that it's not possible to live your dreams. We get up every day and go to a job we hate, or at least are just tolerating, because we have bills to pay. We need health insurance. We have to put food on the table. We believe that our dreams won't pay the bills. We tell ourselves that this is reality. This is real life—dreams are, well, just dreams!

Here is a powerful question from Steve Maraboli: "How much longer will you sit back and wait for your dream to spontaneously come true? Too many days, weeks, months, and years have passed! Do not be unresponsive to your own dreams. Now, set a course of action that will lead to bringing your dream into reality."[44]

That vision speaks about the rewards of a life well-lived. It speaks of movement and action. It speaks of faith—believing in yourself and in the gifts implanted inside of you—and that when you sow your gifts as seeds into your life, they will bring many blessings to others. This, my friend, is releasing the river. This is taking center stage as the star of your own story. Walking in our purpose is not just for our benefit. The satisfaction we experience from casting bread upon many waters is not the real goal. It's a side benefit. The real goal is how our life poured out blesses other lives.

But make no mistake, you will be filled with joy. The key is that you must cast your bread on the waters. You can't stand and watch the wind and clouds and expect your dreams to be manifested in your life. Your purpose will not be fulfilled from you just standing and watching. Ecclesiastes 11:1 says, *"Cast thy bread upon the waters: for thou shalt find it after many days."*

The word for *cast* in this verse is the Hebrew word *shalach*. It means to "send away, let go, or stretch out." And think about bread. Bread represents sustenance. We eat bread and food to give us the strength to live. When we cast our bread upon the waters, we are sending forth our energy and strength into the world. We are stretching ourselves, stepping out of our comfort zone and challenging ourselves to grow into the fullness of who we are meant to be. It's basically a picture of letting go of your life force to feed others. But the coolest part is that it comes back to you. You are fed, too. You are strengthened and expanded in the process. And you are filled with joy!

DREAMS DO COME TRUE

I was the speaker for a women's retreat, and the location for the retreat happened to be the same place our church held our women's retreats for over a decade. It was kind of a déjà vu experience for me because that exact place was where I had many personal struggles and victories in my journey to taking center stage of my life. Those struggles and victories had to do with speaking and sharing my message and story.

This was the same room where I discovered that inner story that I told you about in Chapter 7. It was a place where I experienced many internal battles with fear and timidity. I didn't think I had what it took to step into the very thing I was created to do—speak into the lives of women, encouraging, teaching, and empowering them to be who they are created to be. It was at those retreats with my church that I finally began to step out and teach and speak.

And here I was again in that same location, fully stepping into my place as a speaker and spiritual teacher—doing what I had been afraid to do. It was incredible. And I don't believe it was a coincidence. It was all part of the design of my unique journey.

One thing I have come to realize is how important it truly is to know and value your destiny. No one else can do what you are uniquely designed to do. Only you can fulfill your purpose. Only you can walk your path. Only you can be the master of your life. Only you can cast your bread on the waters.

Putting yourself out there—all the way out there on the center stage of your life—means completely letting go of pretense and anything holding you back. Is it risky? Yes! Not everyone will like what you're doing. Not everyone will applaud you and cheer you on. But at this point in the STAR Process, if you've done the work, the opinions of others won't matter so much. The only opinion that truly will matter is the opinion you have of yourself—and that comes from seeing who God created you to be and fully embracing His opinion of you.

Only when you let go and put yourself out there on the stage of life will you be able to truly live. Living is about giving— pouring all of yourself out—not going to your grave with your song still inside you!

CLEAR EYES, FULL HEARTS, CAN'T LOSE

There was a television series I was hooked on years ago called *Friday Night Lights*. The story centered around a family living in a small town who loved their high school football team. The father of the family was the coach. He was one of the reasons I loved the show so much because he consistently focused on building the character of each of his players more than just winning football games. The core message was that the game of football and the game of life were best played when you gave your all with clear eyes and a full heart. Before every game, as he gave the team his pep talk, he would say, "Clear eyes, full hearts, can't lose!" This mantra served as a consistent reminder to the players of the power of drive and optimism. It reminds me of the Apostle Paul's admonition to us in Philippians 3, quoted at the top of this chapter. He speaks of running a race, forgetting what lies behind, and pressing forward to the prize—our high calling from God. We can't lose when we keep our hearts and eyes fixed on our purpose and destiny. But to keep going for- ward and not give up, we need perseverance and motivation. We also need a clear vision and a fully engaged heart that is committed to crossing that finish line.

CLEAR EYES

Having clear eyes means that you remove anything that clouds your vision so you can see where you're going. You must know where the goal line is and how you're going to get there. You'll have opposition from the other team. They will try to stop you, knock you down, and discourage and dishearten you. They will try to throw you off your game and confuse you, so you don't know which end is up.

There will always be people who try to dim your light. They don't understand your vision. They just won't get it. That's because it's not their vision or their goal. They want to go another way toward a different goal, their goal. They will think that their way is the best way, and they'll try to convince you of that, too.

You need clear eyes so that you don't get sidetracked and blocked by people and situations that get in your way. You must clearly see your path and go for it with your whole heart.

YOU NEED A CLEAR VISION

You must be super clear and focused on your path and your vision. You must be clear on your value and your purpose so you can see your goal even if you don't know exactly how you are going to get there.

Creating a crystal-clear vision of what you want to accomplish and where you want your life to go is extremely important, but many people struggle with this. You can easily get distracted and veer off that path onto another path before you're aware of it.

I've seen myself speaking from a large stage in a huge auditorium. It's a vision that has floated into my mind at random times over the years. I used to push it away thinking that it was ridiculous and absurd. How was that ever going to happen? Why would all those people come to hear me speak? Who was I to be speaking on a big stage?

But the vision persisted and continued to flash onto the screen of my mind out of nowhere. Finally, I decided to stop pushing it away and take a serious look at it. Maybe this vision was from God. Maybe He was trying to tell me something.

I began to embrace that vision as a possibility. I didn't focus on the when or the how because those were unknowable. And it doesn't matter how or when. I realized that if I was going to cooperate with God and fully put myself out there, I would need to accept this vision as an invitation to pursue the goal of becoming a speaker.

That women's retreat was my first experience as a paid keynote speaker, and that opportunity found me. So, the question changed from "Why me?" to "Why not me?" If this is something God is calling me to do, then who am I to question Him? I began to welcome the vision instead of rejecting it.

VISUALIZE YOUR DREAMS BEFORE THEY BECOME REALITY

In fact, you need to visualize what you want and where you're going before it can manifest in your life. Preparation work must take place within you so that you are equipped. You must receive the vision, believe in it, and then you grow, learn, and develop the character to match the assignment. You've been endowed with huge creative powers to cooperate with the visions and dreams you've been given so that they become a reality.

Visualization techniques have been used by successful people to create their desired outcomes for centuries. We all have this awesome power, but most people don't know how to use it. Elite athletes and the super-wealthy use it. In fact, the most common reason people don't succeed or accumulate wealth is that they don't see themselves doing it. Once you genuinely see yourself as capable of succeeding or making more money or whatever it is God has called you to do, all kinds of things begin to happen. The amount of wealth or abundance in the world doesn't change, but you can tune your radar to the possibilities of bringing more of that abundance into your life.

You are creating a "future memory" when you visualize something. The more detailed the image, the more specifically you etch it into your brain. Your conscious mind must incorporate the mental picture into an evolving story as part of your identity for it to manifest.

When you etch your visualized goal into your brain, it creates what is called "cognitive dissonance." This is the difference between where you are and where you want to go. When you feel like things aren't what they should be, your brain goes to work finding ways to end this tension by bringing into focus the opportunities and strategies that will help you manifest your vision.

Get Your Body into the Vision

I took a course called The Neuroscience of Change. One of the instructors was Amanda Burke, author of *Your Body Is Your Brain*. She taught us how to connect our bodies to our vision when we are visualizing what we want to create in life. In one session, she asked for a volunteer to do a demonstration, and I was the chosen guinea pig. She walked me through an exercise that was incredibly powerful for me. I am going to walk you through it as well.

She asked me to think of something I wanted to do but didn't think I had it in me to do. I chose that vision of me speaking on a large stage in front of a huge audience. I was then instructed to see myself in my mind walking out on that stage as clearly as possible. She asked me what I was experiencing physically as I visualized that scene. I was aware that I felt closed in. My shoulders hunched forward, and my chest caved in, almost like I was trying to protect my heart or chest from a blow. I didn't notice it, but she pointed out that as I described that feeling, my body went into that position. My head also went down into my chest. I was closing in on myself.

Next, she asked me what thought was going through my mind in that moment. The thought was, "Who am I to do this? I don't have what it takes. What am I doing here?" The emotions were anxiety and fear.

Amanda instructed me to notice that feeling and the thought for a minute. Then we took a break from that, and I shook off the feeling and relaxed. I took a couple of deep breaths and centered myself again.

The next step was to visualize walking out on that stage again, but without any fear or anxiety. She asked me to describe what I saw myself doing. Right away, I saw that vision that had come to me for years. I walked out confidently to the center of the stage and faced the audience with my arms spread open wide and a smile on my face.

What was the thought running through my mind this time? It was, "I was made for this!" Amanda asked me to do that same movement and speak that thought out loud a few times. I did, and it felt quite powerful.

Amanda explained to me that if I practice doing that movement and speaking that statement often, whenever I think about it—just walking around my house—my mind and body will connect the thought to the physical movement and to the vision of speaking on that stage. Then when the actual day comes and I walk out onto a big stage, that path will be there in my mind, and my body and emotions will fall right in line with it. It is like rehearsing before a performance. You create these pathways in your brain and your body, and it is quite natural to do it. Your brain and body don't know when it is the rehearsal or the real performance. Dancers, musicians, and athletes all do this. Muscle memory connected to the thoughts and the images in your mind come online immediately when you need them.

Since that session, I have been rehearsing this, and I've even done it on a couple of stages (in empty auditoriums). One day, it will be for real, and my body will be ready along with my mind, my heart, and my soul.

Visions Manifest Themselves in Small and Consistent Action

My speaking vision began to feel real, but there is a gap between where I am now as a speaker and being on that big stage in front of hundreds or maybe thousands of women. I needed a clear vision, but I also needed a plan of action. That vision was not simply going to materialize in front of me one day. I needed clear and specific goals, like steps on that path, that would get me from here to there. And I needed to take those steps and act on the plan.

God expects us to work with Him in walking out our destiny. You can dream all day long and see those visions God gives you, but He is waiting for you to get up and move. Take the next step and the one after that. Your path unfolds before you as you go. You grow, you learn, you develop, and you become stronger and more confident with every step. His power works through you as you take those steps. Along the way, God develops in you the endurance, resilience, and skill you need to realize the fullness of the vision He has placed in your heart.

Zig Ziglar once said, "If you aim at nothing, you'll hit it every time."

What are you aiming at? Is it written down? Is it so clear that you can see it actually coming to pass? Will it bring you the satisfaction of knowing you fulfilled your destiny? Is what you're aiming at what you really want to be doing?

FULL HEART

"If you leave this world with a full heart, then that is a beautiful life. And that's what I want," said Ravyn Lenae, a singer.

A full heart means that you're all in. You've cast all your bread on the waters. Your heart is fully engaged in following your divinely ordained life mission, and nothing or no one will stop you. Your heart is full of faith and love because you believe in your mission and yourself. You are committed to following through to the end, no matter what.

I love birds. I love listening to their unique songs. I love watching them fly. I especially love watching them nest. One year, we had a pair of robins build a nest on top of our front porch light. I enjoyed watching them as the nestlings hatched and grew. The parents were so attentive, always watching over their babies from a nearby tree. Whenever I walked outside, the parents would chirp loudly from their tree warning me to stay away from their babies.

When it was finally time for the babies to fledge, a fascinating and dramatic scene unfolded before me. The fledglings perched on the edge of the nest, flapping their wings, teetering there, seemingly conflicted by their situation. It was time to try out their wings for the first time and leave the comfort of the nest, which they had clearly outgrown. There wasn't enough room there for them any longer. But they hesitated for a while, as if they were trying to decide whether to go for it or to stay. They wanted to take the leap but were not sure they could do it. The parents were in the nearby tree, calling to their babies, urging them to fly. They kept their distance.

Finally, one by one, the babies jumped out of the nest into the big world. The last one to leave flapped its wings awkwardly and made it to the end of our driveway and just sat there. The mama bird landed nearby, clearly unhappy. She chirped sharply and even pecked at her baby as if to say, "Come on. You can do this! Keep flying! Don't give up! You were made to fly!"

In my imagination, she wanted her fledgling to put its full heart into what it was created to do—to make it on its own in this big, wild world. We can learn a lesson from these birds. We've got to go all in. We must trust that we've got this. We were made for this. It's time to go all in—full hearts and clear eyes. Staying in the comfort zone is no longer an option. There isn't enough room there for us. We have grown beyond where we've been, and now it is time to spread our new wings and take flight into our next season. The season in the nest was good and necessary. That's where we developed our strengths and learned new things. Now, we are ready to put them to use by letting go of what was and leaping into what will be.

Some people will tell you to stay in the nest and settle for what is safe and familiar. They may be caring and compassionate friends and family, but they aren't doing you any favors. Listen to the ones who call to you from their nearby tree. They are calling to the greatness within you, challenging you to be your best self and fulfill your highest calling. They are the ones who believe you can do it. They are the people who have taken the leap and spread their wings, and they know what it takes. They are courageous, and they see the courage in you, too.

Answer that call and take the leap with a full heart. It's the only way you'll fulfill your mission on earth.

Use the *Clear Eyes Vision Blueprint* in the **STAR Guide** to help you create your vision for what's next.

You are finally ready to take center stage and be the STAR of your own story!

Access the Digital Workbook: https://bit.ly/StarGuideWorkbook or the Paperback Workbook: https://amzn.to/3JUkchQ

CHAPTER 12

TAKE CENTER STAGE

If we did all the things that we are capable of doing, we would literally astound ourselves.

~ Thomas Edison

Now unto him that is able to do exceedingly abundantly above all that we ask or think, according to the power that worketh in us, unto him be glory in the church by Christ Jesus throughout all ages, world without end.

~ Ephesians 3:2021

FROM MY JOURNAL (AGE 55)

I was standing next to a tiny spring bubbling up out of the ground. After a short while, it sputtered and disappeared as it was sucked back underground. The earth was totally dry for some time until, without warning, a huge pillar of water blasted up into a massive and fiery fountain. I noticed fire in the water. It burned with intensity and a purity I had never seen before. This "fire-water" spread out in all directions as it hit the ground, while the fountain continued to surge high into the air.

As I meditated on this vision, the meaning became clear. My impression from the Spirit was that this fiery fountain represented different seasons in my life. There was a time when my influence and power to touch lives was quite small in its reach, confined to those closest to me. This was followed by a dry season, a wilderness of the soul, during which I went into a secret place with the Lord, in hidden places where there was no outward manifestation of God's work within. It was during a time when I had experienced deep wounding from people I loved and trusted, and this caused me to withdraw. During that time, God worked deep things into my spirit, purifying and refining so that all that I needed or desired was to be in His presence. The desire or need to be approved by others began to fade as my vision of my own worth and value became crystal clear. The seeds of confidence were sown into my heart as my soul grew strong.

As His deeper work created a greater foundation, His power in me intensified until the time came for it to be released. The Spirit whispered to my heart that the deeper I am rooted in the love of God, the greater the power of His love in me to reach others will be. I have traveled through seasons of preparation, but now I am entering a season of release and much fruit. My heart heard these words: "You will have more compassion for the broken, and this fountain from your soul will refresh the weary."

As I pondered this vision and all that my heart received, it occurred to me that this is true of each of us. We are on our own unique journey, with desert seasons where it seems that nothing is happening around us, and we see the dust of forgotten dreams. But as we continue our journey, in faith and trust, we find ourselves in a rich season of blessing and abundance. Each season does its work in our souls and has its part to play in our growth. As we embrace the seasons of our lives and fully experience the gifts they offer, fullness and deep satisfaction will abide within. Each season weaves another thread into the tapestry of who we are and who we are becoming, enabling us to take our unique place in the fabric of all creation.

So, you see, my friend, going deep inside to unclog my fountain produced something far greater and richer than the pain of the process. You may not have had a lot of traumas in your past, but everyone has a past, and most of us have events from our past that we have not processed. My guess is that you are no different.

As you read my story, some past hurts may have surfaced in your conscious mind, maybe even some that you've not thought about in many years. You may feel as I did—that it isn't relevant now. You may be thinking that it was such a long time ago that it has no relevance to your life today. I assure you that if it has come up to the surface while reading this book, it has relevance for your life. It came up for a reason.

If you noticed some things surfacing as you have read this book, I urge you to give your attention to those things. Listen to your heart. Allow yourself the time to unpack those things. Don't stuff them back down and try to keep carrying all that baggage around with you. It's time to let go so you can be free to take center stage in your life. What does that look like for you?

This is what it looks like for me.

About two years ago, I began to recognize something—a new experience of myself. I realized that I finally feel like I am walking on the center stage of my life—as me. Unashamed, unapologetic, unafraid. I can now stand in front of everyone, arms outstretched, no longer hiding behind the curtain backstage. I'm no longer wearing a mask or pretending to be someone else. I am me, and

I feel completely at home in my skin, ready to play my part in the story of the world, not worried or afraid of what the audience may think of me. I am ready to be front and center in my life, fully engaged and alive. It feels so good—so powerful and free and content.

You've heard it plenty of times throughout this book, but what do I mean by the phrase "take center stage"?

The dictionary defines it this way: to be in a main or important position. If someone takes center stage, they become the most significant or noticeable person in a situation. Center stage is the position where actors are most noticeable.[45]

To take center stage in my own life does not mean that I am the most important or significant person in the world. It means that my soul, my real self, is centered inside of me. I am no longer hiding my true self or diminishing my worth and value. I am the most significant person inside my soul as a cherished daughter of God. It means that I am noticing me and accepting me as the unique, valuable human being that I was created to be. It means being centered and grounded inside, no longer thrown off-center by the opinions of others or by my own attempts to be someone else.

The dictionary defines *off-center* to mean "Not centered—diverging from the exact center. Off-center characters who disrupt other people's lives."[46] When I am off-center, I am not myself. I disrupt my life and other people's lives when I am not showing up fully as my authentic self.

Stasi Eldredge puts it this way: *"Becoming ourselves means we are actively cooperating with God's intention for our lives, not fighting Him or ourselves. God accepts us right at this moment, and He wants us to accept ourselves as well. He looks at us with pleasure and with mercy, and He wants us to look at ourselves with pleasure and mercy, too."*[47]

Exactly. Not fighting against who we are, but fully accepting and embracing all of ourselves. That includes accepting and embracing your flaws and weaknesses and quirks. That includes loving your wrinkles, big hips, and crooked smile. That includes loving your personality—whether you are quiet and reserved or loud and exuberant. It means embracing your tendency to be super organized with everything in its place or having piles of papers on your desk and clean laundry piled on the bed for days. It means loving yourself when you make a mistake and when you hit it out of the ballpark. It means knowing your value and worth even when you have a frustrating day and bark at everyone around you. It means no longer beating yourself up and putting yourself down inside your head. It means looking at yourself in the mirror and being able to say, "You're amazing!"

When I turned fifty, I wrote this in my journal: "As we mature, or age like wine, we become more beautiful, precious, and pleasing to Him. We emerge like fine jewels when the dirt of the world and crust of self is removed."

There is a season of emerging that seems to happen in your midlife years. I've experienced it, and I've observed it in many others. You've come through many seasons of struggle and conflict. You've matured like fine wine as you wrestle with the demons of your past and rumble with inner conflicts and fears. There will be times of uprooting old thoughts and beliefs that have been there many years. You find that you need to take a stand against those things that hold you back—things that pressure you to play small and hide behind the curtain where it feels safe and comfortable.

Becoming the star of your own story requires you to become comfortable with the uncomfortable. Taking those first few steps out onto the stage feels risky. The spotlight is shining on you. People are watching you. Some are cheering you on, but others will be jeering at you, booing you, and hoping that you fail.

None of that matters. What matters is how you see yourself. When you love what you see inside, the opinions of everyone else will no longer dictate how you show up on the stage of your life. You will be free to be who you are. There is a peaceful, calm, quiet confidence in that space. Restraints fall away, and you step out boldly and beautifully into your place in this world.

This is a place of release. Releasing the river inside you. It means just being you, walking in fearless confidence, at peace with yourself, genuinely loving who you are. This is not conceit or arrogance. This is seeing yourself as you are, a valuable and unique individual, fearfully and wonderfully created by God.

You look gorgeous there in that place. It fits you perfectly!

Access the Digital Workbook: https://bit.ly/StarGuideWorkbook or the Paperback Workbook: https://amzn.to/3JUkchQ

How Might That Show Up?

It might show up in the discovery of the power of your voice, and you may find yourself speaking up in meetings, like my friend Kathy. I first met Kathy when she joined my women's speaking club. She wanted to work on building confidence in sharing her thoughts and ideas at work in meetings. She felt that no one wanted to hear what she had to say, so she rarely spoke up. Since working on this, Kathy has found herself speaking up more, and her boss has taken notice. In a recent performance review, her boss commended her for her contributions and noted how other team members found value in what she shared. That's taking center stage.

It might show up in the form of being able to own your accomplishments and talk about them to others, instead of hiding them in fear that others will think you are bragging or that you'll come across as arrogant. My friend and fellow entrepreneur, Megan, wrestled with this one when she had the opportunity to throw her hat in the ring to be named one of the top thirty women business owners under thirty by our local chamber of commerce. Megan is doing amazing things in her video agency business and has grown her new company from two (herself and her husband) to a team of seven in only three years. She is incredibly gifted in her work helping businesses to create growth strategies using custom video assets.

Megan was hesitant when it came to talking about her accomplishments. To be in the running for this award, she needed to fill out an application in which she would talk about all her achievements. She felt awkward doing so, as if she were boasting and bragging. I challenged her to write from a third-person point of view as if it were someone else talking about all she had accomplished. It was all true, wasn't it? She wasn't making stuff up. As she wrote, she felt her confidence rise and a great sense of satisfaction knowing that she had shared her gifts and was building an amazing company as a young entrepreneur. She was ultimately named as one of the thirty under thirty award winners because that is truly who she is. Megan took center stage of her life as she owned her accomplishments in a humble embracing of her truth.

Marcy is taking center stage by writing her book and releasing all that has been locked inside her—her story, her wisdom, her passion—out onto the written page. This experience has been healing for her soul, and I have no doubt it will bring much-needed healing to others who read her book.

Allison is taking center stage and has stepped into the world of creative entrepreneurship. She is an artist sharing her art through her subscription service where members receive a uniquely designed and crafted "clothing box" each month. She is daring to show up and share her gifts with others, and she is making a powerful impact as she does so.

Suzanne is taking center stage by putting her innovative ideas into her winery business and watching them expand and grow her customer base. Previously, she would not act on her ideas because she was afraid to take the risk. During her STAR

Process, she discovered her strengths, embraced them, and put them into action. The result has been an increase in her business revenue, her growth as an entrepreneur, and a leap in her personal sense of worth and value. This is fearless confidence.

This is taking center stage as the star of your story.

Other ways taking center stage could show up in real life:

- asking for what you need and want
- charging what you're worth
- going after what you want with gusto and passion
- setting clear goals and laying out your action steps to achieve them
- leading your team—communicating, motivating, empowering them to take initiative, be innovative, and be more productive
- addressing the problems and conflicts in relationships so they can improve
- managing time and being more focused and productive
- taking that class, getting that degree, or asking for the promotion/raise
- creating that product or course or program
- trying new things: scuba diving, sky diving, rock climbing, silks class, paddle boarding, painting, running, biking, hiking, starting a business, becoming a speaker, or learning a new language.

So, my friend, I ask you: How will *you* take center stage and be the STAR of your own story? What will that look like for you?

As we wrap up our time together on this journey, I want to leave you with five key concepts. Write these down on index cards so you can pull them out and review them whenever you need to remind yourself that you are the star of your own story.

1. It's all about inside work. True transformation always occurs from the inside out. Changing inside of you must happen first.

2. Becoming you is a journey, not a destination. Change comes from the process. Trust the process. Stay present on the journey.

3. Your purpose flows from who you are, not what you do. You are living your purpose through every season as you grow and mature into the fullest expression of who you are.

4. Your thoughts are powerful. They create your life. Everything starts with a thought that is grounded in a belief. You choose what you believe, and you choose the thoughts you dwell on.

5. You have greatness inside of you. Potential lies dormant within that seed to become whatever it was designed to be. You have the potential to be you, the absolute best you, right there inside you, waiting to break forth.

We've been on a journey together through this book. I've shared my story and the stories of several other women with the hope that you will gain much insight into your own heart and soul. Your journey is different than mine, but the concepts contained in the **STAR Process** are universal. They call us to go deeper and not to be afraid to know ourselves well.

They serve as mirrors to reflect the parts of ourselves that we've lost touch with along the rocky road of life. They ask us to turn aside and rest, to pause and breathe, and to know that we belong here. We have a place in this world, a significant part to play in the story of humanity. We are here on purpose, for a reason, equipped with all we need to fulfill our mission. Our part is important, valuable, and needed.

It's time for you to see yourself as you really are. You are a magnificent jewel and a shining light of beauty. You are safe. You no longer need to hide who you are. You can shine purely as you in your brilliance and beauty. You no longer need to wear that mask.

Take center stage of your life. Walk out there with confidence. Stretch out your hands with joy, and let your light shine out to all the world. You are the star of your own story. No one else can be. I hope and pray from the depths of my being that you get that. I hope that as you turn the final page of this book that you know you are a STAR. You are magnificent. You are brilliant. You belong.

Be confident. Be real. Be you.

Scan the QR Code above with your smartphone
for my special message about
Be the Star of Your Own Story. Or, follow this link:
https://youtu.be/tb_wPpMXtqk

ABOUT THE AUTHOR

Janelle Anderson is an author, Certified Professional Coach, and renowned speaker who is on a mission to empower women of all backgrounds to embrace their greatness and know their true value. Having overcome a past of sexual trauma, Janelle is dedicated to challenging and encouraging her listeners to find their untapped potential and become the stars of their own stories. She's also the host of the weekly podcast, *Women Emerging Fearlessly*, where she inspires her listeners through the power of stories – stories of courageous women who are taking center stage and shining their light - women who have overcome tremendous challenges to be who they were created to be, so that her audience may be empowered to show up, stand up, and speak up in fearless confidence.

Janelle draws on her faith as a boundless source of inspiration and strength in her life, and she credits God with helping her get through her darkest moments and emerge as a stronger, happier, and more confident person. As the leader of *Speaker Sisterhood Christiansburg* and creator of her signature online course, *Speak Confidently to Sell*, she's passionate about helping other women develop speaking skills and create their unique voices in the world. Janelle currently enjoys the simple life in Virginia with her husband Bob.

To connect with Janelle for coaching or speaking services, email info@emerginglifecoaching.com

Visit her website at www.emerginglifecoaching.com

If you are a podcaster/media/summit host looking for speakers, check out my media kit!
https://www.emerginglifecoaching.com/books

Here are the links for the accompanying workbook.
Digital Workbook Link:
https://bit.ly/StarGuideWorkbook

Here is the link for the workbook:
https://amzn.to/3JUkchQ

Invitation to sign up for the group program:
If you would like to have support, guidance, and accountability as you work through the book and workbook, sign up here to get more information on the Be the Star of Your Story online group program and find out how to enroll.

Be the Star group program sign up link:
https://bit.ly/BetheStarGroup

BIBLIOGRAPHY

Achor, Shawn. *The Happiness Advantage: The Seven Principles of Positive Psychology that Fuel Success and Performance at Work.* New York, NY: Crown Business, 2010.

Attwood, Janet Bray and Chris Attwood. *The Passion Test: The Effortless Path to Discovering Your Life Purpose.* The Penguin Group, 2008.

Bennett, Roy T. *The Light in the Heart: Inspirational Thoughts for Living Your Best Life.* Roy Bennett, 2016.

Betz, Ann and Lisa Feldman Barrett. "Neuroscience of Change Course." 2019.

Bevere, John. *The Bait of Satan.* Lake Mary, Florida: Creation House, 1982.

Brown, C. Brené. *Braving the Wilderness: The Quest for True Belonging and the Courage to Stand Alone.* UK: Penguin Random House, 2017.

The Gifts of Imperfection: Let Go of Who You Think You're Supposed to Be and Embrace Who You Are. Center City, MN: Hazelden, 2010.

Cacioppo, John T. and William Patrick. *Loneliness, Human Nature, and the Need for Social Connection.* New York, NY: Norton, 2008.

Carstensen, Laura L. Ph.D. *A Long Bright Future: Happiness, Health, and Financial Security in an Age of Increased Longevity.* New York City, NY: Random House, Inc, 2009, 2011.

Chen, Robert. "The Real Meaning of Passion." Embrace Possibility. March 2015. Accessed April 15, 2021, https://www.embracepossibility.com/blog/real-meaning-passion/.

Clinton, Robert J. *The Making of a Leader: Recognizing the Lessons and Stages of Leadership Development.* Colorado Springs, CO: NavPress, 1988.

Dictionary.com. "Off-Center." Accessed April 15, 2021. https://www.dictionary.com/browse/off-center.

Urban Dictionary. "Passion." Accessed April 15, 2021. https://www.urbandictionary.com/define.php?term=Passion.

Eldridge, Stasi. *Becoming Myself: Embracing God's Dream of You.* David C. Cook.

Fonda, Jane. "Life's Third Act." January 4, 2012. TedX Talk. 11:20. https://youtu.be/lHyR7p6_hn0.

Griffin, R. Morgan. "10 Health Problems Related to Stress You Can Fix." WebMD. Accessed April 8, 2021. https://www.webmd.com/balance/stress-management/features/10-fixable-stress-related-health-problems#1.

Kelly, Dr. Edward J. "The Third Act: When There Is No One Left to Blame." The Third Act. Accessed April 8, 2021. http://thethirdact.ie/wp-content/uploads/2015/01/The-Third-Act-No-one-left-to-blame.pdf.

Kist, Jane A. G. and Sandra Krebs Hirsch. *LifeKeys: Discover Who You Are*. Minneapolis, MN: Bethany House, 2005.

Leaf, Caroline Dr. *Switch on Your Brain: The Key to Peak Happiness, Thinking, and Health*. Grand Rapids, MI: Baker Books, 2013.

Leaf, Caroline. *The Perfect You: A Blueprint for Identity*. Grand Rapids, MI: Baker Books, 2007.

Maraboli, Steve. *Unapologetically You: Reflections on Life and the Human Experience*. Port Washington, NY, NY: A Better Today Publishing, 2013.

McGhee, Robert S. *The Search for Significance*. Nashville, TN: W Publishing Group, 1988.

Me Too Movement. "Statistics." Accessed April 27, 2021. https://metoomvmt.org/learn-more/statistics/.

Merriam-Webster. "Take Center Stage." Accessed April 15, 2021. https://www.merriam-webster.com/dictionary/take%20center%20stage.

Rath, Tom. *StrengthsFinder 2.0*. New York, NY: Gallup Press, 2007.

Schneider, Bruce D. The Law of Being. iPEC Coaching. 20172010.

Sizemore, Rick. *Wilderness: A Stepping Stone to the Greatness of God*. Christiansburg, VA: Dealing Jesus, 2015.

Stoltzfus, Tony. *Christian Life Coaching Handbook: Calling and Destiny Discovery Tools for Christian Life Coaching*. Virginia Beach, VA: Coach22, 2009.

Wikipedia. "Shame." Accessed April 11, 2021, https://en.wikipedia.org/wiki/Shame.

Wolf, Shannon. "Not Easily Broken: Trauma Bonds and the Road to Healing." Christian Counseling Today, 2021. 4749.

Endnotes

1. Kelly, *The Third Act*, 2021.

2. Fonda, *Life's Third Act*, 2012.

3. Carstensen, *A Long Bright Future*, 2009, 2011.

4. Leaf, *Switch on Your Brain*, 39.

5. Leaf, *The Perfect You*, 40.

6. Leaf, *Switch On Your Brain*, 40.

7. Leaf, *Switch On Your Brain*, Loc. 441.

8. Leaf, *The Perfect You*, 40.

9. Leaf, *The Perfect You*, 46.

10. Leaf, *The Perfect You*, 59.

11. Brown, *The Gifts of Imperfection*, 40.

12. Wikipedia, n.d.

13. Me Too Movement, n.d.

14. Wolf, *Not Easily Broken*, 4749.

15. Bevere, *The Bait of Satan*, 147.

16. Griffin, "10 Health Problems Related to Stress," n.d.

17. Betz, "Neuroscience of Change Course," 2019.

18. Sizemore, *Unapologetically You*, 75.

19. Maraboli, *Wilderness*, 16.

20. Brown, *The Gifts of Imperfection*, 45.

21. Brown, *The Gifts of Imperfection*, 40.

22. Brown, *The Gifts of Imperfection*, 46.

23. Maraboli, *Unapologetically You*, 49.

24. Rath, *StrengthsFinder 2.0*, iii.

25. Rath, *StrengthsFinder 2.0*, 12.

26. Kist, *LifeKeys: Discover Who You Are*, 2005.

27. Stoltzfus, *Christian Life Coaching*, 7.

28. Stoltzfus, *Christian Life Coaching*, 22.

29. Bennett, *The Light in the Heart*, 2016.

30. Clinton, *The Making of a Leader*, 1988.

31. Maraboli, *Unapologetically You*, 44.

32. Maraboli, *Unapologetically You*, 103.

33. Eldridge, *Becoming Myself*, 216.

34. Brown, *Braving the Wilderness*, 2017.

35. Brown, *The Gifts of Imperfection*, 64.

36. Cacioppo, *Loneliness, Human Nature, and the Need for Social Connection*, 2008.

37. Stoltzfus, *Christian Life Coaching*, 111.

38. Achor, *The Happiness Advantage*, 2010.

39. Urban Dictionary, 2006.

40. Chen, "The Real Meaning of Passion," 2015.

41. Stoltzfus, *Christian Life Coaching*, 111.

42. McGhee, *The Search for Significance*, 171.

43. Attwood, *The Passion Test*, xxiii.

44. Maraboli, *Unapologetically You*, 19.

45. Merriam-Webster, "Take Center Stage," n.d.

46. Dictionary.com, "Off-Center," n.d.

47. Eldridge, *Becoming Myself*, 98

WE LOVE REVIEWS!

Made in the USA
Columbia, SC
13 February 2022

55379952R00141